MICHAEL L. PAPESH

Good news PARISH LEADERSHIP

TRUST-BUILDING GUIDELINES, TOOLS, AND IDEAS

TWENTY THIRD 23rd
PUBLICATIONS
www.23rdpublications.com

TO OUR TRIUNE GOD,
Father, Son, and Holy Spirit,
in heartfelt thanksgiving

FOR DAD
whose meticulous instruction about
how to mop the basement floor
without swabbing myself into a corner
fired in me the Slovenian blessed rage for order and
whose professionalism as a funeral director
set a life example that continues to inspire me

FOR MOM
whose native intelligence passed on to me
the wit to be reflective and articulate about my experience and
whose most gracious Irish hospitality
touched me tenderly,
and gifted me with endless longing
for the joys of God and home
intimated in table fellowship

Twenty-Third Publications
A Division of Bayard
One Montauk Avenue, Suite 200
New London, CT 06320
(860) 437-3012 or (800) 321-0411
www.23rdpublications.com

ISBN 978-1-58595-705-7
Library of Congress Catalog Card Number: 2008925305
Printed in the U.S.A.

CONTENTS

Acknowledgments

To claim authorship is to risk hubris because a book, like everything else in life, is a committee endeavor, a group accomplishment. I wish to express my heartfelt gratitude, therefore, to all who share with me this book's authorship.

I wish to extend special thanks to colleague and friend Deacon Bill Umphress for repeatedly urging me to write this book. Without that I would likely not have undertaken it. I am grateful as well to Bill Huebsch, an encouraging and discerning if strict task master, whose insistence during the book proposal stage honed my focus and set me on a happy course in spite of my attractions to the contrary. Many thanks to my folks, Mary Jean and Joe Arado, for hosting me during the writing.

Colleagues Tom Donlon and Mary Adrian provided consistent support throughout the writing process. Tom pushed me to find my voice and keep it. Mary nudged me to deeper perspective and creative breadth. How wonderful to have principals on your side! Bill Umphress's initial list of human resources topics and review of chapter nine buttressed my confidence. My good friend Jodi Auvin did me the great kindness of reviewing the whole text before submission. Her ear for language, eye for error, and gift for style helped me clarify what I really meant to write—thought I had written—in passages throughout the book. Our conversations were humbling and uplifting. Thank you to one and all.

Twenty-Third Publications has given me a great opportunity and most gracious gift by supporting this work and publishing it. I am very grateful to Deborah McCann, who edited the book, Dan Connors, Michelle Gerstel, and Dan Smart for their kindness, advice, patience, flexibility, and generosity throughout this project's completion.

In this silver jubilee year, I also wish to thank the best of colleagues I have known in ministry, as a layman and ordained, as a staff member and as pastor: Marian Walstrom, Gerry Keefe, Butch Rowan, John R. Roach, Roger Carroll, John Bauer, Paul Jaroszeski, Frank Fleming, Kevin McDonough, Bill McDonough, Mary Adrian, Dorothy Paulson, Anne Raiche, Dick Barrett, Bill Umphress, John Barrett, Michael Haley, Joy Biedrzycki, Kathleen Ryan-Huyen, and Tom Donlon. Without these wonderful men and women, who taught and formed me in ministry around the low table of pastoral leadership, and the many others who on staff and in council these past twenty-five years did the same, this work would never have come to birth. I am deeply grateful to God for them all.

Michael L. Papesh
The Western Slope of the Rocky Mountains
frmichaelpapesh@yahoo.com

CHAPTER 1

The Roadmap

» Our Day and Age

We live in an after-council age, a time of massive change, flux, and adjustment in the Catholic Church. Ours is an era when, among the good people on any side of a given question, some think the pendulum swings in their direction and some think it swings against them. All sides are probably correct and mistaken. Decades on since council's end, we remain blinking still from the dust Vatican II kicked up when good Pope John XXIII opened the windows of the Catholic Church to the Holy Spirit's wind and fire.

A former colleague of mine did a doctoral dissertation on the implementation of the great Counter-Reformation Council of Trent (1545-1563). He concluded that it took seventy-five years for Trent's dust to settle. The people who "won" were those who worked hard, stayed the course, and refused to give up. Looking back to that post-conciliar age, we in our own post-conciliar age have no reason to assume that the full implementation of Vatican II will take any less time or grit. Controversy about the council's true interpretation continues to swirl, and

1

will for a good long time to come, vastly complicated by the immense cultural breadth of today's globe-embracing church and the ongoing social upheaval across the nations of the world.

This book offers a model for "on-the-ground" parish pastoral leadership that hopes to help pastoral leaders in the postconciliar Catholic Church in the U.S. coordinate the work of our hands, left and right. Much of the hand coordination weakness we experience as a church today arises from how lay and ordained people understand their respective roles in the church.

We in the U.S. have the most educated, most affluent, most confident laity ever known in the Catholic Church throughout the world and across the ages. The parochial school system established in the nineteenth century Age of Immigration did its job, and it set values, priorities, and aspirations among U.S. Catholics that have brought Catholic men and women to thriving leadership in American society and the global community. Our era is reshaping expectations regarding the laity's role in pastoral leadership.

The differing expectations of right and left, of lay and ordained, however, require us to look straightforwardly, even bluntly, at the reality in which we live day-to-day, especially in the parish, so we might consider how we can best join together collaboratively and collegially in Good News pastoral leadership.

» The World: Created Good

God created the world good, very good. We broke it. Jesus came eating and drinking with sinners. He showed us how to recreate the world good. We broke his body and his blood was poured out. Jesus then showed us the absolute fullness of God's goodness. Giving us everything we need to live within it, he invited us to share a memorial meal where heaven and earth meet in our eating and drinking together so we can taste and see the Lord's goodness and then, nourished by it, spread that goodness to the world. The breakage goes on. Why?

» The Root of the Breakage

Power. Power looks different depending on who exercises it. Some impose their notion of perfection, or what it is to be helpful, or what achievement is; some impress on others their understanding of what authentic self-expression is, or their insistence on being right, or their sense of what's responsible; some push others because of their need to avoid pain, be strong, or keep peace. Power's exercise can be active or passive. It looks different in men than in women, it varies across generations, national boundaries, and cultures. Power most certainly can be wielded for good, yet just as certainly it is the root cause of the world's breakage in the face of God's overwhelming goodness. A friend puts the essence of the problem most tragically when he remarks, "I want someone to love me, hold me and be close, but I want it when I want it and how I want it, and then I want to be left alone." We really do demand that it be our way.

» Power Structures Relationships

God fashioned us in his image and likeness, and gave us the world. We want the world fashioned in our image and likeness. The church burst forth from the wind and fire of the Holy Spirit to be Jesus' presence in the world. We festoon it in finery, make it our presence, and proclaim that. Jesus told us to remember him in Eucharist so all would become him, become Eucharist in the midst of the world. We restrict who eats and drinks and who ought not, and we fuss over the banquet particulars. Thus we remember ourselves in Eucharist, and people like us, thereby leaving the world hungry and thirsty for something more and someone other than just us. All of it is about power.

We human beings struggle all our lives with questions of power. Who is in charge? Who says so? Who does she think she is? Who gave them permission? Why listen to him? We know, too, that power takes many forms as power competes with power. Knowledge is power. Money is power. Education is power. Role is power. Access is power. Talent is power. Beauty is power. Physical prowess is power. Temper is power. Ask a child on any playground and he or she will tell you all about power in relationships: who can play with whom and who can't, who is "in" today and who is "out," who everyone wants to hang with and who no one wants to play with at all. Before the playground comes to be, from the moment the family pecking order rises in our consciousness, we learn that some people have power and some don't, we have power over some things and not over others, some people have control over our lives and some don't. Life is shaped by how power is distributed in human relationships.

» Leadership Distributes Power

"Leader" is the word we use for those who have power, for good or for ill. The Indo-European root word *to lead* is the same as the root word *to load*. The root word carries with it the sense of movement. To load implies carrying the burden loaded. To lead is to show the way or direct the course, and implies being on the move. Leadership takes us somewhere. As he or she shows, guides, commands, or directs, a leader bears the burden of moving others by distributing power—the leader's power and the power of the group.

Think of the early part of the Exodus story from the Egyptian perspective. Pharaoh wants his supply cities built. Pithom and Raamses probably serve the whole people, but they most surely immortalize Pharaoh, who is content not merely to subjugate, but to enslave a people to get what he wants. When Moses and Aaron approach Pharaoh to let God's people go, Pharaoh increases their work, directing the taskmasters and foremen to increase the brick quota and make the slaves get their own straw. The Nile turns to blood, polluting the nation's drinking and irrigation water, but Pharaoh commands the slaves to continue building his monuments. The Egyptians suffer frogs, gnats, flies, pestilence, boils, hail, locusts, and darkness—still Pharaoh demands that Israel work on. The Egyptian people lose their firstborn; only then does Pharaoh relent. Yet, he soon changes his mind and pursues Israel into the desert. Stubbornly, as if in the stranglehold of madness, Pharaoh sends his whole army, all of his chariots and charioteers, down onto the floor of a wondrously split Red Sea so he can get his slave labor back. The flower of Egyptian manhood—fathers, sons, brothers, and friends—drowns and Egypt's national security dies, all because Pharaoh wanted to have his supply cities and personal monuments built. Archaeologists tell us that Pharaoh Ramses II lived on after all this to a ripe old age…while Egypt wept.

Leadership distributes power to move others; it burdens those who guide, direct and show the way. The Exodus story proclaims loudly that leadership's power distribution burdens everyone. Yes, leadership takes us somewhere.

» Humans Want Power Distribution Structured

A household refrigerator offers a case study in leadership power distribution. As I write, I live with my parents. Mom cooks and oversees food storage. Joe, my stepfather, makes soups, prepares daily breakfast fruit, orange juice, and salads, and stores half-eaten sandwiches and half-full glasses of milk or juice in the refrigerator after almost every meal. I prepare my own breakfast daily and occasionally cook pasta dishes, make salsa, or put together a sandwich.

One recent morning I went to the refrigerator to find egg salad for an open-faced breakfast sandwich. I expected it to be on the top shelf, right hand side. I found chicken salad there and some dried beef, a half-empty juice glass, and some old gravy, but no egg salad. I pulled and pushed this and that down all the shelves, then finally found the egg salad on the bottom shelf, left hand side, behind the pickles. I was only mildly inconvenienced. Nonetheless, I told Mom the story later that morning.

"The refrigerator is hopeless!" she blurted. Then she reported that she never knows if the milk will be on the door or not, and that while the vegetables are supposed to be in one humidifier drawer and the meat in the other, inevitably she finds the meat among the vegetables and vegetables in with the meat. "If you can't keep that straight, what can you rely on?!" she quipped.

At that moment, Joe walked into the dinette. "We're telling refrigerator stories," I informed him.

"The refrigerator is hopeless!" he blurted. "You can't find anything you want in there!" We all laughed, then told more stories.

None of us can easily find anything in the refrigerator. Each of us is somewhat frustrated, yet no one is willing to exercise leadership enough or respect someone else's power distribution in such a way that we *can* easily find things in the refrigerator. Mom wants to lead but has given up. Joe stores food however he pleases, thus asserting a form of leadership, but gets frustrated when it's not exactly where he puts it, all the while refusing to respect Mom's sense of order. I simply guess where things ought to be and often put them there, but stay out of the fray because… well…I presume I have no power over their refrigerator.

How wonderful life would be if one of us would lead regarding refrigerator food storage and the rest would respect his or her distribution of power! Unfortunately, none of us sees the importance of refrigerator order enough, wants to exercise leadership enough, or is willing to accept another's leadership enough to do that. So we all live with the mess and whine about it. Could it be that if we agreed to let Mom set the order, respected her order, and took the occasional reprimand for a goof, then we could all find things? Imagine! Sometimes leadership takes us to a dead stop, and we stoop to rearguard action so we survive.

Whether it be the family refrigerator or Egypt, we human beings look for someone to lead, to distribute power among us, and so bring order to life. Sometimes we resist because we don't care enough, trust someone enough, or want things our way, so we accommodate and live with the messy refrigerator. Sometimes we follow the in-place structure no matter what—blindly or because we feel coerced—and people fall or drown left and right. There are times, of course, when leadership takes us forward in such harmony that the refrigerator stays orderly for months on end and Pharaoh governs his people conscientiously with a wise justice. Whatever happens, leadership (or its failure) directs life's events and movement; leadership power distribution (or its failure) determines the outcome.

Throughout history, therefore, human beings have structured leadership by setting expectations and making rules for its exercise so power will be distributed effectively. Ancient Greece and Rome did that, and so did eighteenth-century American colonists. Ancient Israel did that, and so did Islam and the Mormons. Children do that on the playground, and so do young people on the dance floor, men pouring a foundation, and women organizing a neighborhood garage sale. The church does that, too.

» Church Leadership and Power Distribution

The purpose of church leadership, its leaders' distribution of power, is to transform the world according to the pattern of life Jesus has shown us. As the church's base community, the parish's mission is to proclaim God's goodness to the world, be God's goodness in the midst of the world, and spread God's goodness to the ends of the world. Yet, very often even in the parish, leaders exercise power not for the common mission but for themselves, and so the refrigerator remains a mess. Very often even in the parish, the distribution of power erects monuments to the "me" who leads, leaving expectations unmet, rules broken, and the field piled high with casualties.

A CASE IN POINT

> Fr. Joe pastors four little parishes: St. Michael, St. Gabriel, St. Raphael, and Guardian Angels—commonly referred to as the All Holy Angels Catholic Community (AHACC)—scattered across territory the size of Rhode Island. He came to the parishes with twenty years experience of being a pastor in one small parish, at an age when most Americans retire, and in a position of major responsibility in his religious order.
>
> After becoming pastor, Fr. Joe soon realized that the secretary, Dierdre, controls the office and all parish communications, nurtures a wide array of relationships across all four little communities, and holds strong opinions about what the pastor ought and ought not do. A simple man, yet wise and wily, Fr. Joe decided to move his office out of the parish center and into the rectory so he could avoid conflict and preserve his power. He has succeeded. Parishioners, however, think him inaccessible and unavailable because when you call the office, all

I must distinguish carefully between two aspects of the role the Lord has given me, a role that demands a rigorous accountability, a role based on the Lord's greatness rather than my own merit. The first aspect is that I am a Christian; the second, that I am a leader. I am a Christian for my own sake, whereas I am a leader for your [the people's] sake; the fact that I am a Christian is to my own advantage, but I am a leader for your advantage.

» ST. AUGUSTINE, SERMON 46

messages, even on the answering machine, go through Dierdre.

Because of Fr. Joe's commitments to his religious order and the enormous time they take away from his being at the parishes, he requested that the multi-parish pastoral council expand to include the heads of all parish clubs, organizations, and committees. Council meeting time is now given over to hearing reports so the pastor gets basic information about the parish. The structure leaves those who come to the meeting swirling in a mix of facts and opinions, unsure about the relative importance of any given ministry because all get the same treatment. Does the AHACC have ministry priorities or not? The council has precious little time to do any work beyond reports. This move, too, preserved Fr. Joe's power.

All acknowledge that Fr. Joe is indeed the AHACC pastor. He has preserved his power. No clear ministry direction, however, emanates from the too busy and well-insulated pastor or from the flabbily structured council. Volunteer ministers in each of the little parishes work hard to hold the individual communities together and do the best they can. Parish-wide gospel ministry, however, fails to cohere, and forward movement in the parish is stymied. A messy refrigerator!

A SECOND CASE IN POINT

Eight years into his pastorate, after five years debt free and consistent efforts to build community trust, Fr. Jordan and the parish leadership agreed to erect a 32,000-square foot addition onto the school building. Fr. Jordan agreed with the finance council that there would be no change orders. He kept the building committee small, however, so he could control construction details. He also privately asked parishioners to donate significant sums to fund religious art throughout the new building.

As the addition neared completion, a trustee learned about a thirteen percent increase in expenses because of change orders and the unexpected religious art. Piqued, he went public with it at a parish meeting that ended in near catcalls directed toward the pastor. The trustee lost his post, council members departed, rumors flew, the new building dedication was a bust, trust was broken, and the momentum of Fr. Jordan's pastorate stopped dead, though he remained on his horse, like El Cid, for three more years. Egypt was piled high with casualties.

Leadership takes us somewhere, but when Fr. Joe refuses to lead or stiff-arms the folks in order to preserve his power, can the refrigerator still be brought to order? When Fr. Jordan undercuts his leadership and squanders his power, can the dead get buried, the wounded be healed, and the Egyptian people be revived? Can parish leadership be shaped in such a way—can parish power distribution be structured in such a way—that failures like these are blunted or, better, rendered nigh impossible?

» Guidelines, Tools, and Ideas

This book aims to answer those questions in the affirmative by offering guidelines, tools, and ideas for shaping pastoral leadership and structuring power distribution so the parish can enjoy, be, mirror, proclaim, and bring to the world the transforming goodness of God. Indeed, the first principle this work aims to set forth is that the effectiveness of the parish's ministry and the church's mission to the world depends very significantly on how the parish structures its leadership relationships. Effective pastoral leadership and power distribution in the parish finds its motive in the church's mission, its principles in sound theology, its focusing images across our tradition, its practices in common sense, its energy in people working together in common cause, and its ground in the goodness of God revealed to us by the transforming pattern of life that Jesus has shown us.

» The Road We Travel

Chapter 2 discusses the elephant in the room of church life for pastoral leadership: the hierarchical clerical culture. It will explore the ethos of the clerical culture, a fundamental context that needs to be considered by all pastoral leaders, as well as the unassailable power that the priest pastor has in the parish. The chapter reflects on that power, some of its limits, and its implications for the parish staff and community. It will also open up the question of how to limit that power for the sake of inviting wide participation in pastoral leadership among all in the parish.

The anxious and alienated human person in our contemporary American culture longs for meaning and connection with others, and fumbles with how to do it even in his or her own family. In parish life this longing shows itself in people's search for "welcome" and "a sense of belonging." The third chapter will make the case that hospitality is the fundamental ministry of the American parish. Grounded in Jesus' ministry of reconciling meals, in his memorial meal, Eucharist, and in his revelation of our God as Trinity—which offer venerable and compelling focus-images—hospitality transforms people, parish community life, and the world. In our time, rising well above clerical culture concerns, hospitality is the church's primary mission. The chapter will define hospitality and explore the three theological grounding-points and images from our tradition that proclaim table fellowship as our primary ministry, thus helping us to bring together contemporary need with our ancient tradition in a meaningful way. The chapter also lists the eight gospel ministries that organize parish community life. It will clarify the options for organizing the parish's ministries and leadership relationships so they mirror the gospel and fulfill the church's mission.

A pastoral leader gathers people together in groups so they can accept real responsibility for a parish's ministry. Chapter 4 defines the word *pastor* as the church understands it, then discusses what is necessary for the pastor's mindset to shift from that of a Lone Ranger to a maestro and from being Herr Pastor to being a coach. It also discusses the attitudes that expand the pastor's effective ministry leadership: moving from thinking of oneself as the parish bulwark to accepting that a pastor is passing through, from thinking of oneself as field marshal to understanding that the effective pastor is a ministry generalist.

Chapter 5 reviews the basics of a parish's leadership structure and reflects on what an empowering posture looks like for the pastor in relationship to parishioner and staff leadership groups. It ends with the point that the heart of effective pastoring is building trust.

A leader is best when people barely know he exists; when his work is done, his aim fulfilled, they will say: we did it ourselves.

» LAO TZU

Chapter 6 addresses council pastoral leadership in the parish. The task of parish leadership groups is to plan, to sort through the gifts and demands of the parish's relationship with God and to focus, guide, and monitor parish ministry life. Therefore the chapter describes the role of the pastoral council and the administrative council in the parish. Pastoral leadership grounds itself in spiritual discipline. All concerns in parish decision making are governed by the umbrella question: what is it that God wants of us? The chapter reflects on discernment as a major task of the councils, and on what consensus decision making needs to look like. It also discusses the place of confidentiality among pastoral leaders.

Chapter 7 reflects on the role of the pastoral staff and administrative staff in the parish. It discusses what it means to say that the pastoral staff members co-pastor the parish, and suggests what the points of contact should be among pastor and staff members. The chapter reviews what works regarding pastoral staff meetings. Since pastoral staff members themselves have advisory pastoral leadership groups, the chapter considers the function of these groups and what they ought to look like. The chapter ends with a consideration of varied parish contexts and how staff relationships might best be structured within them.

One of the places in the parish where heaven and earth meet in the wind and fire of the Holy Spirit is around the pastoral leadership meeting table. Chapter 8 offers perspective on the central importance of the low table leadership meeting, its content and process. It offers rules for meeting conduct. Effective pastoral leadership requires highly refined listening skills, mental agility that brings ideas together, and the humility to let go of one's own biases, so the chapter describes the qualities of the astute meeting chair and offers some thoughts on effective meeting mechanics, including prayer.

Parish life in the United States invariably includes three cultural conflicts. American society's expectations often clash with church values in the areas of decision making and employment. Chapter 9 discusses where the conflicts are and how to strike a workable balance between American and traditional church values in leadership structures and decision making. It also clarifies employment limits and the value of following employment law carefully while keeping employment relationships collaborative, healthy, and trusting. Chapter 10 explores the creative tension that arises in the cultural conflict of a parish's having a school ministry, and it offers a perspective on how to live well within it.

A fundamental question that all of us ask is: will this work? Chapter 11 suggests the possibilities and limits of what a parishioner pastoral council member, a pastoral associate, or a pastor can do to shape Good News pastoral leadership in the parish.

Chapter 12 offers a particular case study—the clustered community of All Holy Angels Catholic Community—so the reader or a pastoral leadership group might apply their own sense of the possibilities and limits of what a parishioner pastoral council member, a pastoral associate, or a pastor can do to shape Good News pastoral leadership in the AHACC. The chapter also offers one perspective on how a pastoral council member, pastoral associate, or pastor might approach leadership in the AHACC.

Four appendices are offered at the end of the book as a kind of toolbox. The reader or a pastoral leadership group will find there useful tools to help clarify and implement Good News pastoral leadership. Guidelines and ideas are scattered throughout the book as well.

» Good News Pastoral Leadership

The Catholic Church in the United States is limping these days. The sexual abuse scandals here and abroad have shaken us. The bishops, content that the situation is fixed and presuming everything is back to normal, have neglected to take meaningful responsibility as a group, continue to gloss over the consequences of ongoing news about hundreds of millions of dollars of payout, have allowed church credibility and trust to crumble, and so have let us down. Leadership has indeed taken us somewhere. Dioceses and parishes bear some of the burden of where we have gone.

These days only one third of our people see Sunday Mass as a high value; seventy-five percent did in 1957. There is no single definition of what *regular* Mass attendance means. The young, who seek inspiration and "a charge" in our worship, grow increasingly indifferent to what they experience in church and refuse to buy whole areas of church teaching. For many, faith is uncoupled from church life, participation in church has become not life's core but a lifestyle option, and religious literacy among Catholics weakens. We American Catholics suffer because of bad news pastoral leadership. Yet we are a Good News people. Goodness is integral to our identity as a people of faith.

Goodness is a primary attribute of God: God is supreme beauty, truth, and goodness. The earth, in Genesis, is created good because only good could come to birth out of the word of God. Goodness is also an essential quality of the Christian life. In Jesus, we are recreated good, coming to birth again in the risen life of the Lord. In Eucharist we are nourished in goodness, and so the goodness of God pulsates within and among us as a people.

Human goodness is grounded in the goodness of God. When we say that a person is good, for instance, we mean that that person is grounded in God, that his or her words and actions in large measure flow from of God, that his or her life expresses the goodness of God and that his or her life bears its fruit in the risen Lord. Moral goodness—the goodness of our actions day in and day out—is but one aspect of God's goodness. To say that a person is good is to say simply, accurately, and most profoundly, that that person is "friend of God"—the greatest of gifts in our tradition, the gift that activates all the other gifts of the Holy Spirit.

God has created us good. Jesus has recreated us good. Eucharist nourishes us in goodness. The Good News calls us to say "yes" to God's goodness and our own, and to spread it within the parish, and from there to the neighborhood, other parishes, the ecumenical community, the civic community, and the world. As we examine pastoral leadership in the parish, a key foundational element for the success of that mission, we have every reason to hope as a community of faith that we can all share in wholesome and healthy pastoral leadership, build and keep trust, and thereby exercise Good News leadership for the sake of the Good News, the church, and the world.

What follows are guidelines, tools, and ideas aimed to equip us all for continuing Jesus' mission to the world, for going where Jesus has shown us…where we really and truly already are, if we will but accept it.

— PROCESS EXERCISE —

Reflect together on the leadership system in your parish's life and on its many pieces: for example, pastoral leadership, consultation groups, the parish office, councils, committees…

1. If you take it simply at face value, what does the structure of your parish's leadership system teach you is the pattern of life Jesus showed us?

2. Taken at face value, what does the shape of the whole relationship system in the parish, and its pieces, teach you about leadership and power distribution in your parish community? What's power for?

3. How does parish leadership establish and hold "the vision" for your parish community? Where is the weakness of that? the strength?

CHAPTER 2

The Elephant in the Room of Church Life

» Power in the Church

Across two millennia of history, in service of the Good News, church leadership has distributed its power and taken us somewhere—and that has included taking leadership itself somewhere. Among the myriad developments that have occurred across this venerable history are those that have given rise to the particular shape pastoral leadership takes in Roman Catholicism: the hierarchical structure of its clerical caste system. Because there are those among us who maintain that this structure is sacred and immutable, even "from the Lord," no reflection on Good News pastoral leadership can skirt the question: what's possible for pastoral leadership in an ancient communion whose power structures are essentially hierarchical?

I very much like the twelve-step movements' image of the elephant in the room. The elephant's ungainliness strikes me as the creation of a committee that couldn't quite agree on how all the pieces fit together. At the same time, the elephant is temperamental and formidable. When it's in the room, you have to engage it, accept it as it is, and work with it to see what's possible. Though many try to do so, ignoring the elephant in the room holds enormous risk. This is a most apt image for the Catholic Church's clerical culture.

» The Clerical Culture

"Welcome to the Club!" With these words a Midwestern bishop exchanged the sign of peace with each newly ordained presbyter during the ordination rite. It was 1965, and I was a fourteen year-old seminarian listening in on the new priests' conversation after the ceremony. They seemed both embarrassed and tickled by the bishop's remark. This exchange alerted me to the clerical culture.

In those days, I saw comfortable rectories with linen and silver on the dining room table, and a footstool under the place set aside for the bishop. I saw French cuffs, dressing for dinner and the pastor in a smoking jacket. Priests were welcomed freely into all manner of people's homes, gifted by cut rates on meals and goods, offered trips and cars.

The relationship structures especially were very attractive. Priests young and old participated in a large web of what seemed to be congenial and respectful relationships. They lived in groups of two and three in rectories, gathered for Confirmation and Forty Hours dinners, toured within the diocese and traveled across dioceses, visiting, vacationing, playing tennis, and golfing together. They remained jocular even when they swapped occasional horror stories about this or that pastor. For as remote as the bishop seemed, I could hear in the stories that he not only shared this life with his priests, he participated in more of the same nationally and internationally with other bishops.

To my young eyes these were striking signs of respect, security, and achievement, beyond what I could imagine in another way of life. It was, for a brief time in my life, part of the appeal of ordained ministry.

» The Clerical Culture Lives On

Many today think that those days are gone, but culture evolves rather than halts. Though many of its externals have changed, the essential clerical culture remains alive and well. For example, in 1965 the typical parish had an older, single woman who lived in the rectory and cooked, cleaned, and did laundry for two or three priests. Today many priests live alone in multi-room rectories. Some have offices and meeting rooms in them, others are home for the priest alone. Some priests today live in their own home, townhouse, or apartment. The priest himself typically cooks, does laundry, and maintains the house. The clerical culture's universe of ideas, patterns of relationship and material reality, like all others, has changed. But the culture remains.

A PICTURE

The ordination had been glorious; the Cathedral was full and a hundred priests had come to impose the ancient gesture of laying hands on the newly ordained. The liturgy over, the newly ordained processed to the sacristy. Though they were exhilarated, the heat of the day struck them as they walked. The two who had not worn their cassocks, for all the ribbing they got before the ceremony, were now grateful they wore just their French-cuffed shirt and slacks under their albs. What remained now were the first blessings.

The fifteen newly ordained filed into the Cathedral sacristy and the Master of Ceremonies directed them to the far end. When the bishop came in, they applauded. All warmth and smiles, the bishop passed the M.C. his crosier and miter, adjusted his zucchetto and took his place on the Roman purple velvet kneeler in the sacristy center. Each new priest in turn, hands folded, went to him at the kneeler and, in hushed tones, gave the bishop a first blessing. After each blessing, the bishop took the new priest's hands into his own and kissed them. All were deeply moved by the tenderness of the moment, touched by the bishop's regard for their order and for them personally.

PARSING THE SCENE

This scene is a classic in the clerical culture. It is an important one for the pastoral leader to parse and understand. Why? *Co-Workers in the Vineyard of the Lord: A Resource for Guiding the Development of Lay Ecclesial Ministry* (CWVL), published by the United States bishops in 2005, answers that question by articulating the lay ecclesial minister's place in church ministry. The texts apply to any lay person's place in ministry.

> The lay ecclesial minister is called to a function in the Church, not to a state of life as happens in Ordination. Lay ecclesial ministry is exercised in accordance with the specific lay vocation, which differs from that of the ordained ministry. (p. 11)

> Lay ecclesial ministers find their relationships with the community and its pastors in the recognition and authorization they receive from these pastors. (p. 25)

> While they differ essentially, the ordained priesthood and the common priesthood of the faithful are ordered to one another and thus are intimately related. Lay ecclesial ministers, especially those serving in parishes, look to their priests for leadership in developing collaboration that is mutually life-giving and respectful. (p. 27)

In these texts the United States bishops are clarifying that the status of lay pastoral leaders is different-in-kind—not in *degree*, but in *kind*—from that of the ordained, and dependent upon the ordained. Plainly put, the bishops are saying that church ministry is a family business and lay people are welcome to serve…but they are not quite family.

In light of this institutional understanding of reality, the picture above offers a telling illustration of the clerical culture. The hand-kissing scene has about it muscular elements not only of sentimental piety, but also of power politics.

Traditionally understood, the hands of the priest are anointed to touch the host; they are sacred and venerable. The anointing proclaims as well that those ordained into the clerical culture are set apart, special. However, isn't it self-serving for one with anointed hands to make a grand gesture of kissing another's anointed hands? The kissing gesture proclaims that the culture is inbred, enmeshed. Everyone in the culture is closely bound, and the boundaries between them are both set and pliable, depending on the circumstances.

Among the orders of the ordained, the presbyter is beholden to the bishop. In the ordination rite this is depicted by the presbyter folding his hands within the bishop's folded hands in an ancient gesture of fealty that pledges obedience. Isn't the punch of the hand kissing precisely the power-reversal as the one to be obeyed makes himself subservient for a brief moment to the one who obeys? This power-reversal gesture has about it a subtext of manipulation as well: "If I would kiss your hands, what wouldn't you do for me!"

This pregnant clerical culture event was a staple of the church prior to the mid-1960s, though the hand kissing was rare and private. This scene, however, occurred in all of its particulars at noon, May 28, 2005. More amazing, the hand kissing was

pictured in the diocesan newspaper. The identical gesture—
the bishop on his kneeler holding the young priest's hands and
looking up into the newly ordained man's eyes, both in smiling
conversation—has been published in ensuing years as well.

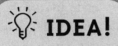

IDEA!

Study and reflect together on the symbolic significance of and connection among

- the presidential chair in the parish church,
- the bishop's throne in the cathedral,
- and the chair contained in the sculpture above
  the Altar of the Chair in St. Peter's Basilica at the
  Vatican.

Do so in light of the prayer texts and readings for the
Feast of the Chair of Peter, celebrated February 22.

Share together experiences of when you have seen
the clerical culture in action.

This picture teaches the pastoral leader a critical lesson: real
responsibility for shaping a faith community's life and ministry
demands that the pastoral leader's relationship to the set aside
and deeply bound together members of the clerical culture be
attentive and sometimes even catering. In order to consider
pastoral leadership's context fully, therefore, we need to consider power and the clerical culture: what power means and what
hurdles must be jumped in order to come to Godly right order
in distributing power for the sake of gospel ministry.

» Cultures Coming Together in Power Relationship

The power differential between the lay pastoral leader and a priest-pastor is unequal as it is institutionally structured. The bishops say so in *Co-Workers in the Vineyard of the Lord*. The lay pastoral leader's status in the church rests in baptism, and his or her ministry is a function. The priest's status rests in holy orders, and his ministry is a state, an ontologically changed life. Consequently, the cleric in a ministry setting, from an institutional point of view, automatically has more power and the lay person less.

Second, practical experience suggests that what lay and ordained ministers have in common is that they are both caught—to a greater or lesser extent, depending on a variety of circumstances—in an enmeshed system. Lay and ordained are both beholden to the clerical culture, and clerics within it, for their position, their security within it, and their ability to exercise pastoral leadership.

A CASE IN POINT

When Fr. Florian became pastor of Our Lady on the Hill, he inherited a church building that had a series of architectural problems: awkward entries, an out-of-sight and useless baptismal font, and an invisible Blessed Sacrament chapel. After consultation with artists, architects, and liturgy professionals, Fr. Florian decided to make several changes that, for a minimal investment, would correct the problems and, in the process, significantly enhance worship for the assembly and trust within the parish. Fr. Florian won approval from the pastoral and administrative councils as well as informal diocesan worship office approval. He published what would be done and why to the parish at large, and major benefactors in the parish fully funded the whole project. The parish began the work.

Fr. Florian's predecessor, however, had become vicar general of the diocese and had never fully let go of being pastor.

Three months into construction, Fr. Florian received a letter from the bishop asking him to halt the project and apply for formal Chancery approval. He did so. Two weeks later he received a letter from the bishop telling him that the projects would need to be indefinitely deferred.

Suspecting the vicar general's involvement in the stoppage, but in an effort to win him over, Fr. Florian met with him to ask his help with the bishop. The vicar general said he would talk with the bishop. A week later Fr. Florian received a letter from the bishop telling him that a committee of liturgical experts from the seminary, the Chancery, and a local parish would be established to review the projects. He would accept their recommendation. Ten days later the committee visited the church. Fr. Florian toured them and made his case.

Nine days later Fr. Florian received a letter from the bishop. Noting that a former associate pastor had met with the committee in its final deliberations, the bishop wrote that he accepted that priest's view that the church needed to remain untouched. The letter concluded that the project would need to be brought to an immediate close, and the money given back to the donors or redirected to debt reduction.

It is a staple of the clerical culture, however, that every chancery's walls have ears. Fr. Florian learned that the vicar general had openly spoken against the project at the Chancery very soon after it began. He had also insisted to the committee, over its protest, that the former associate pastor, who had been at the parish when the church was built in 1955, meet with it to explain the building's original intent. Fr. Florian also learned that the final committee report submitted to the bishop had dismissed what the former associate offered as out-of-date and, with some nuance, recommended to the bishop that the project be completed. The vicar general, however, overruled the committee. Moreover, though the bishop had signed them, the vicar general had written all the letters Fr. Florian had received and controlled the whole process from beginning to end, evidently with the bishop's benign approval. Fr. Florian's resigned assessment after all this political maneuvering was, "Well, at least I was obedient and stayed standing for four months."

Because of the nature of the clerical culture, pastoral leadership requires all who would minister in the church to be attentive and sometimes catering to clerics within the system. We are all of us, in other words, working in a family business. The lay pastoral leader is not quite family, and the ordained pastoral leader can never be precisely certain whether he is family or not because that depends on who has what power in any given situation, and how he wants to exercise it.

So, to understand the opportunities and hazards of laity and priests exercising pastoral leadership together, we need to reflect in a forthright manner on the priest-pastor's power.

» The Priest-Pastor's Power

Co-Workers in the Vineyard of the Lord offers this reflection on the priest-pastor's power.

The diocesan bishop entrusts to the pastor of a parish the responsibility of providing pastoral care to all within the parish, under the authority of the diocesan bishop and with the cooperation of other priests and deacons and the assistance of the laity (Can. 519)....The pastor thus has great latitude in organizing parish resources to meet the pastoral needs of the people. The support of the pastor has been found crucial to the success of lay ecclesial ministry within parish communities. This suggests that although the diocesan bishop may oversee the authorization process, the unique role of the pastor in selecting those who will serve on the pastoral team should be acknowledged. (p. 63)

Because a fresh priest-pastor is aware of these things, he arrives in a parish assuming he has almost complete power. An experienced pastor knows, however, as lay pastoral leaders know, that such an assumption is false. Still, a priest-pastor does come to a parish with significant power.

THE POWER OF ORDINATION
Esoteric Power
Ordination confers mysterious, esoteric power. The priest-pastor walks into the parish authorized to bless and preside at sacraments. If he presides with strength and grace, and blesses with graciousness and purpose, the pastor is immediately accorded even more power than ordination itself gives him. Nonetheless, in the vast majority of instances—outside of the sexual abuse of minors, habitual and hard-hearted crassness, and out-and-out theft—the priest's hold over mystery, his esoteric power, is an enormous power uniquely his. Though it may be flaccidly exercised, it is rarely compromised.

The Power of Preaching

Ordination includes with it the authority to preach. Along with reverent prayer leadership, meaningful and inspiring preaching wins minds and hearts. But as we all know, Catholics have low expectations for preaching. While the good preacher dazzles, the bad preacher little compromises his power in a Catholic setting unless he is a heretic, his behavior grossly contradicts his preaching, or the preaching is utterly empty. Even then, many of the faithful wait a long, long time before making a judgment. Aside from a pastor's grossly contradictory behavior, Catholics remain remarkably indulgent about preaching.

THE POWER OF OFFICE

Pastoral Care

Appointment as pastor means being entrusted with the pastoral care of a faith community, the whole of it and all of its particulars. The pastor is accountable to the bishop and only in an amorphous way to the people, a simple fact, however unsatisfying this may be in an American context. The pastor is nonetheless expected to have a listening ear and sensitive manner with Mabel in hospice and Uncle Herbert at the wedding banquet, with the demanding widow during funeral preparation and bungling Billy the server, with the guys at the ball field, the Women's Club at tea, and the pastoral staff professionals.

Most pastors are uneven in their pastoral care largely because of personality differences both in the pastor and in the parish. Steadiness and consistency, though, count immensely. A pastor's power usually builds in a community by virtue of mere presence at functions and personal sincerity. Only transparent insincerity and consistent absence will undercut a pastor in the area of pastoral care.

Ordering the Ministries: Corporate Officer

The pastor is also entrusted with ordering the community's ministries. In this area that pastor's power is both least assailable and most vulnerable.

On one hand, the pastor is a corporate officer—the CEO— entrusted with all matters of personnel, law, finances, and property. Not only is the pastor's signature required for corporate acts, the nature of the position is such that the pastor can act without corporate approval and, legally, the act will stand. Moreover, the clerical culture will generally wink at most misconduct, if there is any, out of its instinct for self-preservation. Money mismanagement stories, for instance, both deliberate and fumbling, are legion in every diocese. This corporate power for the pastor, then, has its limits, but it is as complete as raw power gets.

Ordering the Ministries: Leader

At the same time, because ordering the ministries requires leadership—that hardly definable quality of a person who inspires and comforts, directs and paces, listens and nudges along, initiates and responds, takes care and takes risks, brings together and separates—the ordering of the ministries is, paradoxically, where the pastor has least power when walking in the door. A pastor needs to earn leadership stripes, and history, skill, relationships, patience, and wisdom will make or break a pastorate.

The contradictions a priest-pastor has to hold together in this area abound: he is accountable within the clerical culture for ministry outside it; he is shepherd of the flock and corporate CEO; he is broadly trusted yet lives under enormous expectations; he wants relationships in ministry but is obliged to caution; he is called to simplicity but essentially lives in privilege; he is a moral authority in public yet serves a clerical culture that privately winks. Other contradictions vex a priest-pastor's life as well, some personal and some professional. Priests are prepared for priesthood but not for pastoring. They are promised to a way of prayer that is nigh impossible to follow. They are sent to proclaim the truth that sets us free, yet in every room sit the elephants of the Vatican, the bishops, the seminary, the ordination of married men, the ordination of women, the fractured clerical culture, and now homosexuality and the priesthood. Pastors are assigned to give their all and then, when they move, to totally let go. They are ministers of unity in a fractured church.

Each of these contradictions, and more, can compromise a pastor's power. We have all seen and heard abundant examples of pastors who have undercut their leadership.

ALWAYS GIVEN THE BENEFIT OF THE DOUBT

As one ponders all the many pitfalls of a pastor's role, three points are especially worth remembering when a priest is pastor. A priest's esoteric power holds him in a unique position and he remains highly valued in the faith community. That esoteric power, especially if seriously and sensitively exercised, trumps almost any other power exertion in the faith community. Second, a pastor's corporate executive power is just short of absolute. If he fumbles it, he will be protected by the clerical culture. Even if he is guilty of misconduct and is removed— rare and extreme—precisely why he leaves typically will be kept secret. The clerical culture allows little satisfaction to ousters of any kind. Finally, because of the nature of his role, and the support he receives from the faithful and the clerical culture, a priest pastor retains power by merely staying in place. As a friend of mine once told me in a tough situation, "Mikey, sometimes the guy who wins is simply the guy who sits in the saddle longest." He's right, and pastors know it. The faithful are very forgiving of their priests and most always give them the benefit of the doubt.

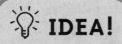

IDEA!

Study and reflect together on the institutional model of the church offered in Avery Dulles, S.J., **Models of the Church: Expanded Edition** or on the contradictions section offered in Michael Papesh, **Clerical Culture: Contradiction and Transformation**.

Share together experiences of when you have seen the clerical culture in action.

» The Priest-Pastor's Sharing Power

It is a fundamental premise of this book that if the priest-pastor is to build and keep trust in the parish community, then he must step aside from clerical culture assumptions in the way he leads with and among the pastoral leaders of the parish. If he is to be an effective pastoral leader himself in our time, then the priest-pastor must implement his broad institutional power in a generously disciplined way that honors the dignity of all, ministers in solidarity with all, stimulates the participation of all in the parish's ministry and governance life, and respects carefully and in a discerning way the principle of subsidiarity, allowing everyone around him to offer the fullest ministry they can without his interference. In the face of enormous pressure to act to the contrary, the holy restraint through which a priest-pastor empowers the whole community to share in pastoral leadership is a rare but crucial gift, and one that parish pastoral leaders deeply cherish.

The clerical culture struggles to understand the model of pastoral leadership this book will lay out. For instance, when he was installed as pastor of Our Lady of Consolation, Fr. Leo was asked to say a few words at the end of the Mass. He took that opportunity to introduce the pastoral staff to the assembly, explained to the people that the pastoral associates shared his pastoring ministry and briefly summarized what he meant by that. When he sat down, the bishop took the microphone and quipped, "Fr. Leo, if all of these wonderful people on your staff are doing such beautiful ministry here in the parish, just what is it that *you* do?"

As rock bound as hierarchical structures are in the Catholic Church's polity, and as entrenched as the hierarchical mentality is in the clerical culture, our venerable Catholic tradition is far broader and richer, deeper, higher, and wider than the clerical culture. If our community of faith across the world would but strive to mirror the pattern of life and pastoral leadership that Jesus has shown us—his reconciling ministry, the essential meaning of his Eucharist, and the life of the Trinity he has revealed to us—then Jesus himself shows us the way to receive, accept, bless, and express a new paradigm for pastoral leadership even in a hierarchical church.

— PROCESS QUESTIONS —

Think back over your lifetime of parish experience...

1. When have you seen the clerical culture in action?

2. When have you seen the clerical culture moderated?

3. What do you think to be the "mystique" of the priest?

4. Has that changed over the years? How? How not?

5. What impact do presuppositions about clerical culture have in your parish's life?

CHAPTER **3**

Hospitality: Paradigm for Pastoral Leadership

» Leaders Take Us Somewhere

Jesus of Nazareth was a leader who distributed his power and distributes ours. Where did Jesus of Nazareth take us? Jesus took us to the cross, risen glory, and the wind and fire of the Holy Spirit. Jesus took us to one another in word-proclaiming witness and just, loving neighborly service. Jesus also took us to the Eucharistic table as the source, summit, and transforming nourishment for the life of the Holy Spirit among us and the pattern of life Jesus has shown us. Through his reconciling ministry, Eucharistic memorial, and the life of the Trinity he revealed to us, Jesus has taken us into hospitality, into the very life of God, for our sustenance as his holy people.

» Hospitality: Womb of Parish Life

Jesus Christ has revealed to us that hospitality transforms people and the world. On behalf of the local and universal Church, the purpose of parish is to extend Jesus' mission to the world. If hospitality is a primary expression of the pattern of life Jesus has shown us, then we can only conclude that hospitality ought to be a primary expression of our pattern of life in the parish as well. Transformation through hospitality, therefore, is the parish's mission and ministry in the midst of the world.

Parishioners in our time long for what they call *welcome* and *belonging*. The rise of greeters and hospitality ministers instead of ushers, the replacement of the parish hall by the gathering space, Sunday-after-Sunday coffee and donuts, and the relentless busyness of the modern parish all point to the loneliness and longing of our people. At Holy Spirit, a city neighborhood parish in the Midwest, the religious formation ministry hosted the most popular event of the year, a pumpkin carving party. The parish provided pumpkins, knives, beverages and pizza; our families simply showed up, and they came in droves. The pumpkin carving party taught the parish staff that in our time people are unsure even about how to be family together, too busy to pull even simple whole-family events together, and appreciate immensely the convenience of the parish's helping them do what they aspire to do. The ministry of Jesus Christ and the human need of our time call pastoral leaders to understand that, in a thoroughgoing way and on many levels, hospitality is the womb of parish life and, in our time, a crying need.

» Hospitality: What Is It?

Hospitality is a form of human relationship that embodies profound mutuality and equality. Contrary to what we might unreflectively assume, in hospitality the host is in no way superior to the guest, the guest in no way inferior to the host. In hospitality, both host and guest need each other mutually and equally to complete the act. Hospitality binds us in freedom, through which the host freely extends hospitality and the guest freely receives it. Hospitality binds us in security, the security of hospitality graciously given and gratefully received. Hospitality also binds us in mutual need reaching for fulfillment, the host's need to attentively satisfy the guest and the guest's need to be kindly satisfied by the host. By definition hospitality is a profound human act that proclaims God's love and justice, and it is transforming.

Some years ago, I had a morning telephone conversation with my mother. She had hosted a women's group meeting at her new home in a new town the night before—twenty-six women. Every plate and cup matched, she had just enough dishes and silverware to go around, and she received many compliments on the dessert. She cleaned up afterward until midnight, no small thing for a senior citizen who habitually retires by 9:30. When I talked to her, she was so thrilled at the success of the event the night before, so elated at the sense of connection and belonging she experienced with new people in a new place through her hospitality, that she didn't know yet if she was tired or not—the exhilaration of a hostess!

In August, 1990, a friend and I spent three days in a mission among the Maasai, a tribe of nomadic herdsman who live and wander astride the borders of Tanzania and Kenya in East Africa. The first day we went to a Maasai village where the missionary was to teach catechism. After a rugged hour's drive through gullies and fields, we arrived at the gathering place: a wide African plain marked by a single tree.

The first sign of the villagers was actually a sound—the sound of singing wafting across the plain. The singers, a single person alternating with the whole group like a litany, were some thirty villagers coming to greet us. First we saw the women, clothed in royal purple, brilliant crimson and bright yellow, bedecked with the white, red and blue beaded neck disks distinctive of the Maasai. The men, the warriors and elders of the village wrapped in red plaid blankets, carrying spears and staves, followed them. They all greeted us by touching hands, then, singing, they processed us through their village. In each of the three areas of the village, we were invited to take pictures and tour their dwellings as the women sang and danced. Afterwards we processed, with them still singing, back to the tree. There, at the tree, the missionary gave a teaching. Following the teaching, we processed back to the village into the hut of the village leader's son, again accompanied by singing.

In a cow dung hut, seated at two wooden tables among the elders, flies everywhere, we were treated to milk tea with pepper, goat ribs, goat stew on overcooked rice and potatoes, and a soda. We ate out of a common bowl, each of us with a tablespoon. The village elders kept us company, but waited their turn until we were finished. Our table had a plastic tablecloth; the village elders ate off plain boards. We were served the goat, the village elders were not. All the while we ate the women remained outside singing. When the meal was finished, the villagers, still singing, processed us back to the Land Rover. There they touched hands with us and bade us farewell.

My friend and I had no categories for comprehending this amazing hospitality. Though he had been there ten years, neither had the missionary. We were overwhelmed. We had come to visit the poorest of the poor, yet we were extended the most extravagant hospitality we had ever known. We had come to extend a curious friendship, and left feeling profoundly bound to the Maasai because of their gift of hospitality.

Hospitality transforms both host and guest. By its very nature hospitality affirms the equal dignity of persons even as it expresses in accepting and being accepted, in giving and receiving, the mutuality and interdependence we share as human beings. Hospitality celebrates unity in love even as it honors the distinct purpose of each person in the exchange between host and guest. Hospitality is an act of love, of neighborly and self-emptying service; it is an act of justice in which we order our relationships rightly for the sake of building the common good. Jesus extends hospitality throughout his ministry, and then across all space and time, because in hospitality we human beings are transformed in love and justice as we meet one another and God face to face, and are bound as one.

» Jesus' Ministry of Hospitality

Controversy initially rises between Jesus and the religious establishment because of matters of hospitality. The first question the scribes and Pharisees ask Jesus in the Gospel of Luke is "Why do you eat and drink with tax collectors and sinners?" (Luke 5:30). The first question they ask Jesus' disciples in Mark and Matthew is, "Why does he [your teacher] eat and drink with tax collectors and sinners?" (Mark 2:16; Matthew 9:11). The scribes and Pharisees ask their question on the occasion of the banquet hosted in Jesus' honor by the newly chosen disciple Levi/Matthew, the tax collector. Why do they ask it? Because sharing hospitality with someone means accepting, blessing and expressing a bond with them.

Jesus replies, "Those who are healthy do not need a physician, but the sick do. I have not come to call the righteous to repentance but sinners" (Luke 5:31–32). In Matthew, Jesus pointedly adds, "Go and learn the meaning of the words, 'I desire mercy, not sacrifice'" (Matthew 9:13). Jesus' ministry scandalizes the pious because his sharing hospitality with the sinner, the outcast, and the unclean announces that he is bound to them. Keenly aware of what his hospitality means, Jesus fiercely defends the bond of it as mirroring the intent and life of God.

Jesus' eating and drinking with sinners distinguishes his ministry. On six occasions in the gospels of Mark and Matthew, Jesus either feeds thousands or a meal raises the issue of the participants' sinfulness. In Luke, Jesus is at table with sinners eleven times. Once Jesus feeds 5,000 and two meals are resurrection appearances; eight of these meals include active controversy about sinfulness. Jesus teaches more at table in the Gospel of Luke than he does in his Sermon on the Plain. In the Gospel of John, where he enjoys hospitality six times, Jesus replenishes the wine at the Cana wedding feast as the inaugural act of his ministry, he feeds 5,000 as the third of his seven signs, and he extends the extravagant hospitality of washing the disciples' feet as the opening gesture of the gospel's seventh sign. In John, too, Jesus teaches at table more than at any other place.

Jesus of Nazareth's all-inclusive and abounding hospitality, singularly characteristic of his ministry, proclaims the limitless, tender care and infinite mercy of God. Jesus repeatedly uses the occasion of a meal to teach about right order in human relationships, the common bond among us all before God no matter what, our absolute obligation to lift others' shame, and the complete extent of the reconciliation the Father offers us—if we will but accept it. Throughout his ministry Jesus proclaims that the Kingdom of God is a glorious banquet of "juicy rich foods and pure choice wines" (Isaiah 25:6) where the whole world— tax collector and sinner, adulterous woman and prodigal son, whining hostess and cowardly disciple—can receive, accept, bless, and express the full healing, pardon, and peace of God.

» Eucharist: the Hospitality of God

In absolute continuity with the whole of his ministry, on the night he is betrayed Jesus reclines around a low Middle Eastern table to have supper with his disciples. He takes bread, blesses it, breaks it, and gives it to them saying, "Take this all of you and eat it. This is my body which is given up for you." When supper is ended he takes the cup, gives the Father thanks and praise, and hands the cup to his disciples saying, "Take this, all of you, and drink from it. This is the cup of my blood, the blood of the new and everlasting covenant. It will be shed for you and for all so that sins may be forgiven. Do this in memory of me." Thus, as a sacrament of his reconciling ministry to the world, his desire to be bound to the sinner, the outcast, and the unclean for the sake of their healing transformation, Jesus commands those who follow him to extend the hospitality he offers from his table to the tables of all peoples in every age and place.

Around Jesus' Eucharistic table, the body of the paschal lamb is broken once again for our sake in the wheat ground into bread for us. In the grape bled into wine for us, Jesus' blood is poured out once again for our sake. In the taking, blessing, breaking, and sharing, Jesus extends the hospitality of God among us in every epoch and every corner of the earth. Around the Eucharistic table, the source and summit of our salvation, where the human becomes divine and the divine human, we are mystically bound with God and one another as we receive and accept the fullness of God's merciful and healing hospitality. Celebrating and reenacting the hospitality of God among us in Eucharist, we become the Body and Blood of Christ we eat and drink, a people transformed into the hospitality of God, the font of God's own life in the midst of the world.

» The Trinity: Three Bound as One in Hospitality

Through his ministry and memorial, Jesus Christ reveals to all humankind that the essence of divine life is a reconciling, all-inclusive, lavish hospitality. In the process, Jesus manifests to the world the full identity of our God.

You will find on the cover of this book the most stimulating and accessible image of God in our tradition: the fifteenth-century Russian icon by Andrei Rublev entitled *Trinity*. A treasure trove of meaning for our reflection, the icon proclaims not only that our God is a community of persons, but it also offers us the flavor of that community relationship as it depicts the Trinity in table fellowship.

The icon provocatively declares that the Father, Son, and Holy Spirit are bound together in hospitality. The thrones, scepters and royal footstools depict the Trinity's bond in equal dignity. Their all having the same countenance, being winged, and wearing celestial blue tell us of their mutuality in their life together. Their personal focus toward one another illustrates their interdependence and common bond. If you allow your eyes to follow from the far shoulder of the figure on the icon's left, down to his feet, then across to the feet of the figure on the right, then up that figure's body to the shoulder and across the tops of the figures' heads—the whole image bends in this way—you see that the Trinity sits in a perfect circle, which proclaims its absolute unity. The androgyny of the figures proclaims that same unity. The halo and right hand of each extended in blessing proclaims their common mission. Their dress—the Father on the left robed in light, the Son in the center robed in his two natures of earthly blood red and heavenly blue, the Holy Spirit on the right robed in the vital green of hope and life—announces their distinctness in mission. The temple behind the Father, the tree of life behind the Son, and the mountain behind the Holy Spirit, where in the end time the 144,000 assemble whose robes are washed clean in the blood of the Lamb, accent that particularity in mission. The cup of wine in the center of the low table around which they sit, symbol of the new covenant in Christ's blood we and they share, depicts the joy the Trinity experiences in life together.

What is more, this inspired image, which so eloquently proclaims the love and justice that is our God, invites us to participate in the transcendent, eternal bond that is the Trinity's own life. Look at the figures' eyes. The Son who presides over the Trinity's life—"Everything that the Father has is mine," Jesus says at the end of Matthew's gospel, "All authority has been given to me in heaven and on earth"—gazes upon the Father, the origin of all life. The Father, the beautiful one ever ancient, ever new, who "established the heavens" (Proverbs 8:27), gazes across the table to the Holy Spirit. The Holy Spirit, "from of old…poured forth, at the first, before the earth" (Proverbs 8:23), gazes to the open space at table in the center of the icon.

That open space upon which the Holy Spirit gazes is the place at table left for us, for you and for me. The Spirit looks to this open place at table in invitation, bidding us to join the Trinity in their table fellowship, to participate with the Trinity in the divine hospitality.

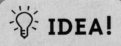

IDEA!

Do a parish-wide retreat that reflects on the three great images of hospitality in our tradition—Jesus' table fellowship, Eucharist, and the Rublev icon of the Trinity—and on the implications of these images for the church and the parish.

The aim of the divine hospitality is the aim of all hospitality: love and justice. In love, the Trinity's hospitality calls us to tender care and self-emptying service. In justice, the Trinity calls us to freedom, security, and the fulfillment of one another's need—right ordering in our relationships. Whenever we extend to others oppression instead of freedom, insecurity instead of security, or want instead of the fulfillment of their need—un-love and injustice—then we withdraw from table fellowship with the Trinity because we are extending to others what is opposed to the Trinity's life of hospitality. We sin. Within the transcendent, eternal bond of their hospitality, the Father, Son, and Holy Spirit perfectly extend love and justice to one another. We accept the Spirit's invitation to join in the Trinity's divine hospitality whenever we strive for the same, honoring the equal dignity of all persons, our human mutuality and interdependence with everyone, and our God-given unity in love and our distinctness in common mission.

» Hospitality and the Parish's Ministries

Following from the pattern of life Jesus has shown us, the central place of hospitality in gospel ministry suggests that food and drink should be the largest single budget item for any parish community. To be church together requires our eating and drinking together. Coffee and donuts after Sunday Mass really matter, and so do cookies and milk at parish meetings, meals at religious education events, dessert at parish club and organization meetings, a champagne brunch after Mass on the parish's feast day, wine and cheese to begin and end the council's round of meetings each year, and pizza or Sloppy Joe's whenever our parish's young people gather. The experience of food and drink hospitality at every parish event ought to be a commonplace, ordinary, expected, most gracious, and downright lovely...always, without exception.

The parish's ministry of hospitality, however, splays out in far more than food and drink. Its overarching expression has a specific and necessary configuration. Parish pastoral leadership organizes itself around eight gospel ministries: worship, religious education, spiritual formation, pastoral care, community building, charity, justice, and administration. These ministries give contour to the parish's extension of the divine hospitality. Effective pastoral leadership structures these ministries in a hospitable way that honors the equal dignity of all persons, human mutuality and interdependence, our God-given unity in love and our distinctness in our common mission. But what does this mean?

The Eight Gospel Ministries

» worship
» religious education
» spiritual formation
» pastoral care
» community building
» charity
» justice
» administration

First, each of these eight gospel ministries requires focused pastoral leadership, whether that be leadership by a person or a group, so all of them will be fulfilled in a parish's life. The parish offers complete gospel ministry only if it extends the pattern of life Jesus has shown us, even if one or another of these ministries is emphasized because of the parish's resources and location. Some of these ministries blend, such as pastoral care and community building or religious education and spiritual formation. Some are thought to blend well with others, but typically suffer in the mix. When blended with charity, justice ministry usually limps. People understand charity in our society; they struggle with Catholic social teaching. Nonetheless, however they might be structured, blended or not, each of these necessary parish ministries demands a host, a person or a group, to focus, guide, and monitor it for the parish.

Second, pastoral leadership in each ministry area must be free to exercise real responsibility. Implementing this principle demands careful structuring for each of the ministries and all of them together. Clearly specifying leadership duties and each ministry's mandate is a must. Avoiding ministry overlap helps enormously, and implicitly invites every ministry's host to reflect on what collaboration among the ministries might look like. Drawing parameters for decision making not only assists pastoral leadership to mold and shape the ministry effectively, it also helps keeps harmony among all the ministries. A cautionary note: Everyone needs to understand that the primary pastoral leader of the parish will need to be informed and consulted regularly about each of the ministries, because additional limits and singular sensitivities can sometimes have an impact on particular activities and concerns. Still, the pastoral leaders of the parish's ministries must be entrusted with real responsibility for the parish's ministry life. The careful shaping of ministry structures and drawing of leadership boundaries accomplishes this goal.

Organizing effective worship leadership, for example, calls for especially careful attention because worship is historically shaped, theologically momentous, artistically sophisticated, richly organic, and yet highly specialized. If a pastoral staff member leads this ministry, then the ordinary presider and that person need to reach a clear understanding about the extent and parameters of their respective roles. Many a priest considers himself a liturgist whether he is capable or not. Consequently, where he ends and the pastoral leader begins (and vice versa) needs to be worked out. Because interest and investment shift from one occasion or liturgical season to another, worship ministry leadership usually works best when a single staff person collaborates with the presider. Still, hospitable pastoral leadership entrusts the worship staff—however it is shaped—with independent responsibility, professional respect, and personal support at every turn.

If a group assumes worship ministry leadership, with or without the guidance of a worship staff person, then prudence demands that the group's responsibilities be carefully delineated. I have rarely experienced effective worship committee leadership. The structure worked when the committee made decisions about big-picture policy and ministry training, not sanctuary environment or Sunday hymn selection. One well-meaning committee insisted that the priest purify the chalices at the altar immediately after communion. The weekend assistant preferred to purify the chalices after Mass and continued to do so; the pastor was unwilling to enforce the committee decision because he was indifferent. Several bumpy encounters finally resolved matters, but the process was awkward and tense for everyone. Ill-defined plans or the tendency to micromanage responsibilities lead to stepping on toes, power clashes, and hurt feelings all around. The extent and limits of any ministry's group-based leadership need always to be carefully spelled out.

Third, those who focus, guide, and monitor a parish's ministry need to be educated and formed to do so. Leading the worship ministry requires study in the areas of liturgy, sacraments, history, and the arts. Religious education leadership demands study of the general and national catechetical directories, basic educational principles, the difference between education and formation, and sound theology. Effective leadership for the parish council and finance committee requires broad information sharing about the parish itself,

the philosophy behind its administrative shape and mana-
gerial style, and various matters of personnel practice, law,
income-expense patterns, and accounting practices. Effective
and hospitable pastoral leadership trusts people and equips
them so they serve knowledgably, competently, and well. Lack
of education and formation hobbles leadership; withholding
relevant information paralyzes it.

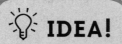

IDEA!

Gather the parish staff and council in a retreat setting and reflect on the gospel ministries:

- Is each of these ministries alive in the
  community?
- Has some form of leadership been established for
  each of them?
- If establishing pastoral leadership in a particular
  ministry is not feasible at this time, how might
  this ministry be raised to greater consciousness
  in the parish until it can be established?

Fourth, every parish complains that lines of communication among pastoral leaders and leadership groups get untied
and dangle, leaving pastoral leaders and groups disconnected
from one another. It is critically important, therefore, that information about each ministry's leadership activities ties *back*
in prompt and clear communication to the primary pastoral

leaders in the parish—the pastoral leader (or canonical pastor), the parish council, and the finance committee—and ties *across* to other pastoral leaders and leadership groups. A larger parish usually keeps its information bonds tied through the pastoral staff, a smaller one more informally. In either case, a publicly known and widely understood information-sharing structure that honors people's ministry responsibilities will maintain clarity about basic information exchange, parameters for discerning future direction, and helpful communication about ministry plans. Lack of information tie-back and tie-across undercuts pastoral leadership and ministry effectiveness, and it compromises resource allocation and parishioner participation. Sloppy bonds, or lack of them, build silos, dribble necessary communication through cracks, and blunt gospel ministry.

Finally, consensus decision making motivates participation, stimulates commitment, inspires motivation, and enkindles trust. Spirituality, the discernment of spirits, needs to govern pastoral decision making. Top-down and majority-rule decisions hit and miss. Some like them, others don't. Group consensus, on the other hand, gradually nurtures unity and builds common vision in a community.

A CASE IN POINT

In 1978, the student coordinators of the volunteer program at the then-College of St. Thomas met to discuss whether volunteer positions in the program ought to receive academic credit for their volunteering. Fifteen people immediately said yes. One woman said no. For two hours she argued her case back and forth with the group on the basis of program integrity and what God wanted of the group as a group—in the midst of tears

Five Fundamentals for Pastoral Leadership

Hospitable pastoral leadership...

 » is focused
 » exercises real responsibility
 » is educated and formed for leadership
 » ties information back and across leadership structures
 » makes its decisions by consensus

and strain for herself and everyone, frankly. In the end, she won everyone, unanimously, to her point of view. The process was long, tough and amazing to watch, but the group ultimately committed itself with deep satisfaction to what everyone firmly believed was the right decision: no academic credit, ever. Thirty years later, the original student leaders long gone, the policy remained in place and so did the volunteer program. Had the majority ruled, what might the outcome have been?

Hospitable decision making binds people, not splits them. It honors the equal dignity of all, relies on the mutuality and interdependence of all, accepts our God-given unity in love, and respects distinctiveness in our common mission.

Focused pastoral leadership exercising real responsibility preserves the bonds among all the parish's ministries and makes decisions based on consensus—these are the fundamentals of pastoral leadership in every faith community that lives out the pattern of life Jesus has shown us.

» Hospitality, Sharing the Divine Life

Every parish community gathers at least weekly in what is essentially its banquet hall to celebrate the dying and rising of the Lord and to eat and drink of his hospitality. Though many among us function in this assembly, all of us come as guests. The Lord is the host of the feast. At the same time, in the eating and drinking, all of us host the Lord in the home of our body, soul, and spirit. This exchange of being host and guest in Eucharist nourishes our life and, if we accept the implications of it, extends the ministry of the Lord to the ends of the earth.

Hospitality is the condition of possibility for all else that follows in the Christian life. It proclaims God's love and justice as it transforms us and the world. It affirms the equal dignity of all of us even as it expresses, in the accepting and being accepted, in the giving and receiving, the mutuality and interdependence we share. Hospitality celebrates our unity in love even as it honors the distinct purpose each of us has in the exchange between host and guest. Hospitality is an act of neighborly and self-emptying service, as well as an act that orders our relationships for the sake of building the common good.

Jesus extended lavish hospitality to the people of his time, and continues to extend it to the people of all ages and times, because of the enormous and transforming impact hospitality has on us humans. That same impact is why the Holy Spirit's glance invites us to table fellowship with the Trinity.

The Good News parish community is first and foremost a place of hospitality. Good News parish leadership calls us all to be attentive hosts and kindly guests at the banquet God lays before us in the parish community and every day of our lives.

— PROCESS EXERCISE —

1. What does it suggest for your life and for the parish that

    a. our God is a community that shares a life of hospitality?

    b. the ministry of Jesus was preaching, teaching, and eating reconciling meals with sinners and outcasts?

    c. the central act of our faith is eating a meal together called Eucharist?

2. Hospitality transforms people. Ponder, and then share: When have you been deeply touched by an experience of hospitality? What was the occasion? What impact did the experience have on your life?

3. What are the strengths and the challenges that strike you as you consider the hospitality you experience across your parish's ministry life?

4. How effective is your parish at implementing the five guidelines for hospitable pastoral leadership outlined in this chapter: pastoral leadership is focused; exercises real responsibility; is educated and formed for leadership; ties back and ties across; and makes its decisions by consensus?

CHAPTER 4

The Good News Pastor

» Trust-Building Pastoral Leadership Relationships

The complexity and breadth of a parish's gospel ministries, the extent of contemporary pastoral need, and our culture's relentless enticements place heavy demands on a pastor. Busyness dominates most pastors' lives. Moreover, lay staff significantly outnumbers priests in US parishes; even two-thirds of the family parishes (200 households or less) are likely to have at least a secretary and a director for religious education, if only perhaps one priest. Well over ninety percent of parishes have councils. Frs. Barry Fitzgerald and Bing Crosby no longer minister alone in the parish, and Sr. Ingrid Bergman, aged considerably, more likely serves as DRE or Pastoral Minister than as a teacher in the school, if there is one. None of them would quite know what to make of the significant pastoral leadership the parishioners exercise, either. So, how do pastor and parish structure pastoral leadership so it works effectively?

Trust-building pastoral leadership begins with the pastor's willingness to step beyond a Lone Ranger, Herr Pastor mindset into one of maestro and coach; it expands with the pastor's accepting that he is but passing through the parish and is strongest as a generalist; and it finds its sustenance in the pastor's hospitable, power-sharing posture with the parish's lay leadership and staff. This chapter will draw the general outlines of the implications of these dispositions for the pastor and the parish. The next chapter will explore the details of how to set up the structure.

» The Term "Pastor"

First, however, it would be helpful to clarify some terms. In accord with ancient tradition, The Second Vatican Council's *Decree on the Ministry and Life of Priests* (DMLP) states that priests, technically *presbyters* who form a college called the *presbytery* around the bishop, are coworkers with the bishop for the purpose of fulfilling the apostolic mission to the world (DMLP, chapter 2). The role of the presbyter is to assist the bishop in his ministry of teaching, sanctifying, and governing the life of the Church. From among the members of the presbytery, after due consultation, the bishop selects pastors (*Code of Canon Law*, 524).

THE INSTITUTIONAL UNDERSTANDING OF THE PASTOR'S RESPONSIBILITIES

Following the Vatican II document's outline, the 1983 *Code of Canon Law* describes the pastor as the shepherd of the parish entrusted to him (Can. 519). All parishes are assigned to a presbyter pastor (Can. 517), even if he is pastor of several parishes and another person under his aegis assumes day-to-day pastoral leadership. The pastor is obliged to announce the word of God through preaching and catechesis; he is to promote the gospel by just and charitable works, oversee the education of children, and evangelize. He is also to see to it that the sacraments are devoutly celebrated and that the Eucharist is the center of the parish assembly of the faithful in every way. He is obliged as well to stimulate family prayer and knowledgeable, active participation in the sacred liturgy (Can. 528). He should strive to come to know the faithful and share life with them, even as he needs to acknowledge and promote the proper role of the lay faithful in the church's mission (Can. 529). The pastor also represents the parish in all legal affairs and is charged to oversee the parish's goods (Can. 532).

THE PRACTICAL SITUATION IN THE U.S.

The United States has around 19,500 Catholic parishes. Some 9,600 of these parishes have one resident priest pastor. Around 3,500 parishes lack a resident pastor. These parishes are largely in the Midwest (1/4 lack a resident pastor) and the Upper Plains (1/3 lack a resident pastor). They are, for the most part, family parishes (200 or fewer registered households) or community parishes (201-549 registered households), as opposed to mega-parishes (over 1200 registered households) or corporate parishes (550-1200 registered households). A parochial administrator—a deacon, religious, or layperson who formally takes the place of a pastor in about 600 of these parishes—is bound by the same duties and enjoys the same rights as a pastor (Can. 540).

TERM DEFINITIONS

Consequently, when this text uses the word *pastor*, it refers to the primary pastoral leader of the parish whether that person is ordained, religious, or lay. The use of the term *pastor* also assumes that the person in the position has all of its canonically assigned rights and responsibilities. One might always read the term in the text that follows to mean pastor/administrator.

The term "pastoral leader" refers to an individual entrusted with any form of leadership responsibility in the parish beyond that of pastor, including paid or volunteer staff as well as council, commission, or committee chairs or members. In some cases this leadership might even be informal. The term "pastoral leadership" refers broadly to groups or constellations of groups entrusted with any form of pastoral care for the parish community.

» Mindset: From Lone Ranger to Maestro

The pastor's mindset has an enormous impact on the tone, pace, and relative effectiveness of the parish's pastoral leadership relationships and most everything the parish does. If the pastor assumes the posture of a lone ranger, then the entire parish's ministry patterns will likely mirror that.

LONE RANGER

Fr. Archie is retiring from being pastor of Sts. Peter and Paul, a large urban parish, after thirteen years at the helm. Pious, kindly, and a good preacher, Fr. Archie has a servant's heart. His vision for the parish is "that the name of Jesus be known and loved." Unable to translate that into practical terms and defensive about it, Fr. Archie nonetheless came into his pastorate surrounded by people so taken by his apparent holiness and charm that they were happy to do that work. Unfortunately, Fr. Archie held his cards very close to his chest. For thirteen years the staff, and the parishioners by way of rumor, heard Fr. Archie's repeated refrain, "Remember, I am the pastor!" In the teeth of that refrain, staff took to jockeying for favor and bending to what they assumed to be Fr. Archie's desires. He allowed a few initiatives, but rarely supervised or followed through. Power vacuums were filled by favorites whom Fr. Archie trusted but the rest of the staff held in suspicion. Though Fr. Archie was fiscally undisciplined, no one had the courage to keep facing him with the bare facts and their implications since that would have led only to an argument and the refrain.

As Fr. Archie's pastorate at Sts. Peter and Paul came to an end, the parish budget was cut by one-third, all full-time staff members were offered a severance package because their positions were financially unsustainable, and staff members who had labored long and well left exhausted, grieving, and resentful. They enjoyed Fr. Archie's Friday homemade soup lunches and his inquiries about the health of their mothers, but they walked out the door uncertain about the genuineness of his care for them. Fr. Archie might have invited Sts. Peter and Paul's leadership to join him in tweaking the strong ministry structure he inherited. Instead, he left disconnected pieces of it in shambles for his successor. Posterity is unlikely to remember much more about him than the simple fact that Fr. Archie was pastor.

On the other hand, if the pastor's mindset is that the pastoring ministry is done within and among groups of people rather than alone, and the pastor intentionally structures it to work that way, then staff feels affirmed and respected, consensus around a vision builds, volunteers rally and parishioners offer amazing time and creative energy in service of the community. A maestro pastor can accomplish almost anything.

MAESTRO

Fr. John inherited three city neighborhood parishes that

...it terrifies me to think that I could take more
pleasure in the honor attached to my office,
which is where its danger lies, than in your
salvation, which ought to be its fruit. This is
why being set above you fills me with alarm,
whereas being with you gives me comfort.
Danger lies in the first; salvation in the second.

» ST. AUGUSTINE, SERMON 340

had bumped along for twenty years in a cooperative relationship. He worked with the councils—four of them,
one for each and one for the whole—to help the parishioners see that three church sites within a mile and a half
of one another were untenable in the long term. Eventually the councils agreed to merge the parishes into one.
The pastor and councils together established processes
for winning diocesan approval, combining funds, co-
alescing staff, selecting a new parish name, arranging
the ritual closing of three sites, selling two sites, money allocation, extensive reconstruction of one site, the
permanent placing of artifacts from all three churches,
and wide dialogical communication with the whole parish throughout it all. The brilliant touch in the process
was a "question box" in which parishioners, identified
or anonymous, could submit their concerns. The pastor promised they would be published in the bulletin
unedited, along with his answers. Mean-spirited questions accompanied by balanced, clear answers shaped
by the pastor and councils garnered enormous sympa-

thy for parish leadership and broad commitment to the merger. It took seven years to complete, but the patient, highly participative process of the merger gradually won over the vast bulk of parishioners to what is one of the most unenviable tasks of contemporary parish life: dissolving multiple communities into a single happy one.

Lone rangers hurt the communities they lead. A maestro pastoral leader gathers people so that leader and group together can accept real responsibility for a parish's ministry and develop consensus about its identity and vision.

» Mindset: From "Herr Pastor" to "Coach"

Underneath the five fundamentals for pastoral leadership offered in the last chapter, then, lies a sixth fundamental: pastoral leaders gather people together in groups to exercise their leadership responsibility. Pastoral leadership is essentially a group experience, not a solitary one. Though leadership methods vary across the ages, and style varies from leader to leader in our own time, pastoral leadership in the church has always been understood to be a group experience.

THE EARLY CHURCH

In the Acts of the Apostles (2:1–12), the Holy Spirit descends in wind and fire on the disciples. The precise number present remains unclear, but the text suggests the group likely includes Jesus' mother, his brothers, and some women, perhaps 120 persons in all. Further on in Acts, although James and Peter significantly shape the outcome, the apostles and presbyters as a group reach agreement among each other and with the whole church about opening the mission beyond Judaism to the Gentiles (Acts 15:1–29). In Acts, the Holy Spirit descends on and operates in groups. This pattern is roundly affirmed in Acts 15:28, where the letter from the apostles and presbyters at Jerusalem to the Gentile Christian community at Antioch begins: "It is the decision of the holy Spirit and of us not to place on you any burden beyond these necessities..." That wording is stunning.

COLLEGIAL MINISTRY

From these early events forward, the church understands that pastoral leadership in the church forms a college that gives unity and continuity to church teaching, beginning with the bishops. Even when Pius IX in 1858 and Pius XII in 1950 make formal infallible declarations—including the solemn declaration of infallibility itself in 1870 amidst thunder, lightning, and the shattering of stained glass at St. Peter's—that exercise of papal authority occurs after wide consultation among the world's bishops and in the midst of a great assembly of them. Indeed, the basilicas of St. Peter and St. Paul Outside-the-Walls commemorate these three events prominently with a permanent display of massive chiseled granite panels that list in stone the bishops in attendance.

A Sixth Fundamental for Pastoral Leadership

Hospitable pastoral leadership...

» exercises its ministry in groups

Authoritative and consultative bodies across the church—from ecumenical councils and synods of bishops, through diocesan presbyteral and deacons' councils and diocesan synods, to the parish council and finance committee—mirror this same sensibility. Pastoral leadership centers itself in groups. There, in the group, the Holy Spirit inspires, animates, directs, and leads the church among those gathered to open themselves to his presence and power. The Herr Pastor pastoral leader, therefore, misses and fails an essential element of who we are as church. Even cardinals have been known to agitate discreetly against papal action when the Herr Pastor pattern takes hold.

NOT "MY POWER," BUT "THEIR POWER"

Consequently, a first concern of the Good News pastor is to empower the people among whom he ministers to lead. The pastor can take for granted the office's institutionally established authority. Building trust requires that the pastor focus his energy on equipping the people of the parish to fill their proper role in the parish's governance and enabling the staff of the parish, along with parishioners, to fulfill their proper role to serve and witness in gospel ministry for the sake of and on behalf of the church's mission to the world.

The pastor is likely to find the people of the parish hungry to lead, but lacking clarity about their boundaries for leading and shy about exercising their role. Many parishioners are intimidated by the church and pastors, and lack even basic information about how the church works. Their suppositions are far more informed by American than by church experience, so their outlook about leadership is usually noisy and confused from the perspective of the gospel and ecclesial tradition. A pastor willing to coach the parishioners into an effective exercise of their leadership, and honor that exercise, ignites gifts in parishioner leadership that can fire the whole parish community to a new sense of mission and deep participation in it.

The pastor is likely to find the staff similarly hungry to lead, but hampered by ideological and personal agendas that have arisen from disillusionment and hurt acquired in their past ministry service. Staff members are typically wary of the pastor's authority, preoccupied about their job security, and less than fully trusting. A pastor willing to receive their gifts as they are, accept them, bless their ministry, express his thanks, and work together with the staff to honor their leadership and help them further hone it, nurtures life in staff members that can blossom forth in remarkable teamwork, glorious creativity, and amazing plain hard work to spread the gospel and serve the parish.

The pastor who coaches instead of demands, and encourages instead of insists, extends a rich hospitality to parishioner and staff leaders. This hospitality, over time, transforms the minds and hearts of everyone involved. As it gradually takes hold over the whole parish community, this hospitality is an important key to transforming parish life.

» Leadership Expansion: Not "Bulwark," but "Passing Through"

Most pastors serve a term of office; at the bishop's discretion they are usually appointed for a specified period of time. In many cases that period of time is twelve years, extendable for good reasons. As mobile as the people of our nation are, many among the parishioners participate in a particular parish's life far longer than any given pastor, and some participate for generations. These simple facts tell us forthrightly that the pastor is not the bulwark of parish life; the parishioners are the parish's past, present and future. These facts require that the pastor shape pastoral leadership ministry not for the short run but for the long haul, and for the parishioners, not himself.

A CASE IN POINT

Fr. Cassian heard teachers and parishioners over the years ask for an addition onto the school building. He passed the request off because year after year the budget was tight and he judged that a capital campaign was beyond both the parish and himself. In the classroom building one day for a fire drill, however, Fr. Cassian watched the children trip and stumble over one another and a boy on crutches because the stairway was rickety and narrow. The drill took twice as long as it ought to have taken. He took his concerns to the councils. Together, within three years, the school addition was a reality and funded. Under the pressure of a genuine safety concern and with hearty parishioner support Fr. Cassian was able to get beyond his reserve and offer the parish long-haul leadership.

Every parish has its own personality and culture. Even adjacent city neighborhood parishes significantly differ from one another because their unique contour is shaped by parishioner personalities and economics, by the style and priorities of former pastors, parish history, and even by the specifics of their location. A pastor cannot grasp, even in twelve years, the fullness of a parish's personality and culture.

A SECOND CASE IN POINT

Fr. Benedict was pastor of a 900-registered household, city neighborhood parish in the Midwest for eleven years. The plant was next door to a seventy-five-year-old, highly respected Catholic high school. Parishioners regarded the elementary school as first among the parish's ministries because of their investment in getting their children enrolled in the high school. For the same reasons they were also content to accept second class status in the use of parish property when the high school's needs demanded that.

Nine years into Fr. Benedict's pastorate, a parking lot use dispute with the high school—he insisted that the lot be cleared of coach and player cars to accommodate parishioners for Masses and that the high school honor their use agreement with the parish, which owned the lot—roused a sleeping lion in the parish that fractured it. Legally and morally Fr. Benedict was right. Politically and practically, however, he had failed to understand the parish's culture and took inadequate advantage of wise parishioner counsel. For the remainder of his pastorate Fr. Benedict was forced to remain ever alert to the roused lion, and the community fracture never did get properly set for its healing.

Because the pastor passes through the parish community only for a time, effective pastoral leadership requires broad collaboration of pastor, parishioners, and staff. This stimulates the pastor, people, and staff alike in their growth toward a richer understanding and ever-fuller exercise of gospel pastoral leadership, even as it helps them to understand the mystery of the parish's history, personality, and culture. This mutual benefit, arising from everyone's graciously accepting the constantly shifting roles of host and guest, builds trust and strengthens everyone's commitment to the main engine for fulfilling the parish's mission: not the pastor, but the parish community.

» Leadership Expansion: Not "Field Marshal," but "Generalist"

The magnitude of a pastor's responsibilities, the complexity of the modern parish's demands, and the aggressive allure of our culture block even the possibility of the pastor exercising full control over a parish community. The pastor cannot master adequate skill, attend to sufficient details, live comfortably within enough relationships, or spend the necessary time it would take to make the parish "the pastor's show." Pastors try, but fail.

A CASE IN POINT

When Fr. Biff inherited St. Damasus parish, power was distributed widely. He pulled it in. He introduced himself to the worship staff as the liturgist. Today, while the music ministry is effective because of its director, liturgy planning is spotty and last-minute. He hired a new DRE to implement his theological perspective, but has been known to dress the DRE down publicly and behind his back upon learning what particular programs look like. Fr. Biff told the councils that he is dissatisfied with their structures and wants to reshape them, but his doing so has fallen by the wayside because he lacks the time, energy, and commitment. He has been clear with the principal that he wants the school ministry to be more Catholic—a school with an already strong religious studies curriculum that includes a service component, extraordinarily plentiful and beautiful religious art in the environment, a faculty that is almost completely Catholic, and a principal deeply sensitive to the dignity of every child, parent, and faculty member. When the principal asks Fr. Biff what he means, he responds, "I am not sure, but I'll know it when I see it." Pastoral leadership uniformly reports that Fr. Biff wants control of everything at St. Damasus, and manipulates to keep it. However, because he lacks an articulate vision and follow-through, the ministries end up flying by the seat of *his* pants.

A SECOND CASE IN POINT

Fr. Jay inherited a parish that his predecessor controlled with two cronies. Fr. Jay spent his pastorate working hard to distribute power across staff and parishioners. He gave the councils real authority to focus, guide, and monitor the parish's life, as well as plan its future, and he brought real parish problems to them for their consideration. He respected staff expertise and decision-making authority, and consistently supported them publicly, confining disagreements to private conversations. He encouraged several focus group initiatives among school ministry parents and among parishioners as a whole, and the councils used the resulting materials for planning. If people brought forward ideas, councils or commissions processed them and the initiator received direct feedback about the leadership group's decisions. Fr. Jay published the parish's budget, structuring it in a way that made clear what each ministry in the parish cost. He even published his own weekly schedule. He also instituted an annual anniversary celebration of the church's consecration, along with a commemorative dinner, and used the occasion to reflect

The Pastor

» oversees, enables, and monitors all parish ministry service
» oversees, enables, and monitors all parish ministry service
» strives to build consensus on the parish's vision
» equips pastoral leaders for their ministry
» insures that pastoral leaders are set free to do their ministry

together with parishioners on the parish's history as a faith community and the meaning of that history. Over eleven years, ministry participation rose from 250 to 670 parishioners sharing time and talent, the parish retired a $300,000 debt it didn't know it had and then built a new ministry center—including a gym that parishioners had failed to support under two previous pastors—on stewardship pledges alone.

Our day and age calls for the pastor to remain a generalist on staff. This means overseeing the parish as a whole in a respectfully collaborative relationship with parishioner leadership groups. In addition to offering personal pastoral care, it also means overseeing the implementation of all eight gospel ministries in a collegial relationship with the staff members responsible for them.

Remaining a generalist honors the unique position a pastor holds and a pastor's singular perspective. Typically, the pastor knows more people, from more angles, more deeply and more perceptively than any other staff member, at least after the pastor has been in the saddle for four years or more. The level to which the parishioners admit a pastor into their lives at the bedside of a loved one, in funeral preparation, at their dining room table, and in the pastor's office is amazing to experience. The pastor's great strength rests in remaining the generalist on staff, using the natural gifts of being pastor to greatest advantage.

Only one exception can make sense: administration. Whether the pastor likes it or not, or is comfortable with it or not, the position by definition—over and above accountability for the faith and morals of the community—means full responsibility morally and legally, canonically and civilly, for all matters of money, property, law, and personnel. This authority is inalienable. Administration, therefore, can be the natural gospel ministry for the pastor to hold close...but it is the only one.

— PROCESS EXERCISE —

1. How is pastoral leadership a group experience in your parish? Where do you see Lone Ranger-ism?

2. What is the impact on your parish's life of what you see in pastoral leadership? How would you like to see it changed?

3. Where do you see genuinely collegial relationships that offer groundwork for building more and even better ones?

CHAPTER 5

The Pastor within the Parish's Basic Structures

» The Pastor's Role

The role of the pastor in a collegial pastoral leadership structure is threefold. First, the pastor oversees, enables, and monitors the ministry life of the parish as a whole in collegial relationship with the councils and parish staff. Second, the pastor is the consensus-builder who, through the open yet disciplined exchange of ideas, perspectives, and plans, assists the pastoral leaders, the pastoral leadership groups, and the people as a whole to come to common agreement about the shape of the parish's gospel ministries and ministry relationships. Third, the pastor equips the pastoral leaders and leadership groups in their efforts to implement group decisions, and ensures that they are free to do their ministry. The pastor fulfills this three-part role in a collegial relationship with parishioners in the parish's governance structure, and with the parish staff in the day-to-day implementation of gospel ministry.

» The Pastor's Governance Posture: Not "Mine," but "Ours"

The pastoral leadership groups that form the basic governance structure of the parish are the engine that shapes the parish's vision and drives its mission. The parishioner governance groups organize the organization. The Good News pastor participates in these structures in the position's proper role, but also with the pastor sharing as an equal in a consensus decision-making process. When the pastor joins in the consensus established around the parish's direction, rather than outside or against it, that extends a compelling vision to the parish and focuses its mission strongly.

THE CORPORATE BOARD

Every parish is a legal corporation. Its corporate status is one element of the parish's structure that leaves the pastor inalienably responsible for all matters of law, personnel, property, and finances. Though the bishop chairs the corporate board, the pastor serves as corporate CEO. The corporate board is a relatively hidden but fundamental collegial pastoral leadership context for every pastor.

In some dioceses all ecclesial institutions are part of a single corporation chaired by the bishop. For most, each institutional entity within the diocese is a separate corporation. In the typical corporate structure the bishop associates himself with the vicar general, the pastor, and two designated parishioners, who are called *trustees* and function as corporate secretary and treasurer, to form the corporate board. This group is the legal corporation; these five together have the legal authority to transact all corporate business and are legally required to do so. This business includes the sale, purchase, or mortgage of gifts of real estate; the granting of easements; lease or rental agreements;

A Pastor's Inalienable Responsibilities

All matters of...

» finances
» personnel
» law
» property
» faith and morals

stock transfers or sales; major capital improvements or renovations; new construction; major service contracts for more than a diocesan-specified amount, and the borrowing of money.

For the sake of an effective melding of the entire pastoral leadership structure, the trustees need to be integrated into the councils. One trustee, the designated secretary of the corporation, ought to be a member of the pastoral council and the other, the designated treasurer of the corporation, ought to be a member of the administrative council. This distribution of power integrates the corporation into the advisory structure of the parish and keeps the trustees, and therefore the majority of the corporate board, closely informed from all sides about the parish's state and plans. It also gives the trustees an opportunity to make ongoing public contributions to the parish's forward movement. Disassociation of the trustees from council leadership risks various forms of diminishment of the trustee role: breakdown in basic information sharing with them, clergy gang-up on the trustees in formal corporate actions, making light of the corporation's place in governance or the trustees' legal role in it, and undercutting the rightful place of parishioner representation on the corporate board.

THE PASTORAL COUNCIL

One of the two mandated advisory bodies for a pastor is what is most often imprecisely called the parish council. The *Code of Canon Law* specifies that

> ...a pastoral council is to be established in each parish;
> the pastor presides over it, and through it the Christian
> faithful along with those who share in the pastoral care
> of the parish in view of their office, give their help in fos-
> tering pastoral activity. This pastoral council possesses
> a consultative vote only and is governed by the norms
> determined by the diocesan bishop. (Can. 536)

Ninety-seven percent of the largest parishes in the United States
down to 88 percent of the smallest have a pastoral council.

The pastoral council is a consultative body responsible for
advising the pastor regarding the focus, guidance, and monitoring of all parish ministries. Practically speaking, the pastoral
council oversees all parish planning and advises the pastor on
any matters which he brings before it, including matters regarding law, property, finances, and personnel. It has a proper
and necessary place in offering its recommendations on every
matter that would be considered by the corporate board as well
as passing on the yearly budget; the major policies regarding
the focus, guidance, and monitoring of each parish ministry;
the long-range plan for the parish and each of its ministries;
the creation of a new ministry position; and the pastor's yearly
goals and periodic ministry review.

The pastoral council, about which more will be said in the
next chapter, serves as one of two basic contexts for the pastor's
governance of the parish. Because the major task of pastoral
leadership in a parish community is building consensus around
its direction, consensus decision making is integral to the council's effectiveness. Though the pastor safeguards the whole, and
technically retains a veto, the pastor ought to participate fully
and equally in the council's decision-making process so complete, genuine consensus is achieved. The council members also
need to keep confidences so the pastor feels able to speak freely

about any and all matters of concern across the parish's ministry life, and so that the council members themselves feel able to speak their concerns and opinions just as freely.

THE ADMINISTRATIVE COUNCIL

The *Code of Canon Law* states that

> each parish is to have a finance council which is regulated by universal law as well as by norms issued by the diocesan bishop; in this council the Christian faithful, selected according to the same norms, aid the pastor in administration of parish goods. (Can. 537)

All parishes have a finance committee.

Because of the breadth of its responsibilities and its importance in the governance structure, *administrative council* more accurately conveys the responsibility and status of this fundamental leadership group than does the term *finance council*. The administrative council is a consultative body responsible for advising the pastor regarding the focus, guidance, and monitoring of the parish's administrative ministries. It also assumes extensive responsibilities for advising the pastor regarding the areas of property and finances, including budget, endowment, sacrificial, and other forms of giving. Further, the administrative council makes recommendations to the pastor on any matters that he brings before it, including personnel and legal matters. Along with the pastoral council, it has a proper and necessary place in offering its recommendations on every matter that would be considered by the corporate board as well as formulating and passing on the yearly budget and the creation of new ministry positions.

The administrative council, which will also be discussed in the next chapter, serves as the other basic context for parish governance. Consensus decision making is integral to this council's effectiveness, too, since the council's task is to build consensus around the abundant technical concerns underneath the parish's vision. Though the pastor safeguards the process, and technically retains a veto in this council as well, the pastor also needs to participate fully and equally in this council's consensus decision-making process. Here, too, the council members need to keep confidences so the pastor feels able to speak freely about any and all matters of concern about personnel, law, money, and property, and so that the council members feel able to speak just as freely their concerns and opinions.

THE PASTOR AND THE COUNCILS

The councils are the foundational, community-wide, consensus-building blocks for everything the parish plans and does. If the pastor listens well to the council members' outlook and point of view, taking them most seriously as a complement to his own, then the perspective council members offer, especially within the consensus decision-making process, can immensely broaden and deepen the pastor's effectiveness. The pastor's honoring the council members' perspective also builds trust between the pastor and the councils, as well as between them and the parish community.

» The Pastor's Ministry Service Posture: Not "You," but "We"

A collegial structure for a parish's staff also significantly expands and deepens the parish's pastoring ministry. Shaping parish-wide consensus on the community's direction becomes much easier if the pastoral staff joins in the council-established consensus. Implementing the vision, and more thoroughly integrating all the ministries into that implementation, is easy to achieve if the staff ministers collegially. Moreover, through the members of a collegial pastoral staff, the pastor can have eyes, ears, and speech in a wide variety of parish settings—a gift to parishioners and pastor that more than makes up for the inability to bi-locate.

THE PASTORAL STAFF

Remaining a generalist, the pastor entrusts each gospel ministry to a staff member who serves as pastoral staff. That staff member may be a salaried person responsible for pastoral care and community building, a stipended person who leads the volunteer lifelong learning core team that shapes spiritual formation and religious education, or a volunteer who chairs the liturgy committee in place of paid staff. What matters is that each holds real responsibility for at least one of the parish's gospel ministries.

A CASE IN POINT

Fr. Leo, whose installation as pastor of Our Lady of Consolation was noted in chapter 1, raised the curtain on this model of collegial ministry in his remarks at the end of Mass. He introduced each pastoral staff member and articulated his or her responsibility for the assembly. He then told the assembly, "These men and women are my co-pastors. Whenever you are in the company of a member of the pastoral staff, you are in the company of the pastoring ministry of the parish. Whenever one of these people is present in the room, I am present...so please feel free to treat them that way." The assembly laughed, of course, but they got the message. Fr. Leo also won, on the spot, the undying loyalty of the pastoral staff.

A brief word about titles. Because they are an extension of the pastoring ministry, the pastoral staff members ought not to

Organizational Chart

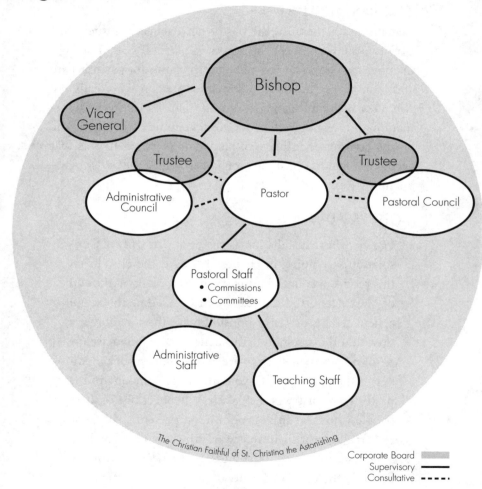

be called *director* of this or *coordinator* of that. Corporate language titles for people with gospel ministry responsibilities mixes metaphors and obscures the deeply significant, transcendent charge with which pastoral staff members are entrusted. The proper title for persons holding major responsibility for focusing, guiding and monitoring a par-

The Pastoral Staff

The members of the pastoral staff share in the pastoring ministry of the parish. They minister in a close, collegial relationship with the pastor and with one another as they...

» oversee and resource gospel ministry implementation
» supervise other ministers
» set and monitor a budget area

ish's gospel ministry ought to be *pastoral associate for* worship, *pastoral associate for* religious formation, *pastoral associate for* business affairs, etc. This titling, using relatively new ecclesial language with a strong undercurrent of time-honored references, articulates well the responsibilities of the pastoral staff members and their relationship with the pastor.

THE ADMINISTRATIVE STAFF

Pooh-poohed by many pastors who profess to be interested in what they call "real ministry," administration is nonetheless an integral gospel ministry. Paul lists it in 1 Corinthians 12:28; the letters to Timothy and Titus are largely focused on administration; the church's ownership of extensive property, and its need for money to maintain it, belies the dismissal of administration as a ministry. Moreover, since ministry may be defined as witness or service done for the sake of or on behalf of the church's mission to the world, those who function in the administrative area of parish life are most certainly ministers. Their ministry belongs to the parish's overarching ministry of justice.

The personal virtue of justice in the Catholic tradition may be defined as the right ordering of relationships for the sake of building up the common good. Consequently, all administrative functions for the sake of or on behalf of the church may rightly be characterized as constituting part of the parish's ministry of justice, notably its stewardship and exercise of subsidiarity. If you have experienced the receptionist talking a suicidal parishioner into calm, the bookkeeper finding the check entry for the ruffled donor, or the maintenance crew getting tables and chairs set up just in time in spite of their having no work request, you know what I mean.

The Administrative Staff

The Administrative Staff comprises those ministers who collaborate together and with the Pastoral Staff to support the gospel ministries of the parish. They function in the areas of...

- » communications
- » finances
- » property management
- » record keeping

The administrative staff of the parish is comprised of staff members who neither oversee a major gospel ministry nor teach in the school ministry. Administrative staff members are charged with parish communications: office reception, the parish website, the parish bulletin, and the pastor's and/or pastoral staff's letters. They manage the parish's finances, which includes keeping track of donor gifts and parish funds, security, bill processing and payment, and preparation of regular, accurate, and transparently sensible reports to parish leadership groups and the parish as a whole. They manage the parish office and its smooth functioning. They manage parish property: keeping the plant tidy—better, sparkling—and in good repair, and serving the space arrangement needs of the pastoral staff. Administrative staff also keeps records of the parish census, the conferral of sacraments (baptism, confirmation, first Eucharist, penance, and marriage), and the death register.

These functions are absolutely critical to a parish's well-oiled running. They require that the pastor have a clear sense of the administrative staff's purpose and communicate with them regularly and often to develop competencies, clarify difficulties, and build trusting relationships.

Another brief word about titles. Because they serve an administrative function, the administrative staff members are appropriately titled in accord with that function. Corporate language titles for administrative staff roles work admirably well. Parishioners readily understand what functions a Director for Finances, a Director for Communications, a Receptionist, or a Kitchen Coordinator perform. The use of corporate titles in this area also distinguishes the charge of the administrative staff from that of the pastoral staff.

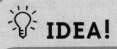

IDEA!

Do a *Basic Policies Book on Governance* with the Pastoral Council and review it with the Administrative Council and parish staff—to help keep everyone on the same page with regard to the parish's basic pastoral leadership structures. See a sample in Appendix I on page 235.

POWER DISTRIBUTION AND PRESERVATION

Leaders distribute power, their own and others'. All pastors, therefore, are appropriately concerned about power distribution in the parish, and they need to be. But the pastor's concern regarding power cannot be for the pastor's position alone. Because the pastoring ministry is a group reality, the nature of the pastor's role demands that the pastor attend to the parish staff's power distribution and preservation, that the pastor model well how to distribute and preserve power, coach staff so they know how to do it well, and occasionally do everything he can to preserve a staff member's power when the going gets rough, as it inevitably does.

A CASE IN POINT

Tom Moore is part-time coordinator for religious education in the sister parishes of St. Perpetua and St. Felicity. Soon after his arrival on staff, he pointed out to the parish secretary that the single page website could be far better used, especially for religious education news. She took his suggestion and engaged Mrs. Tatum O'Rourke, a parish volunteer, to do the website work. Over several months Tatum added website pages for all the ministries, spending hours and hours on the project. Because Tatum seemed overly and inappropriately interested in communicating with him about the website and other religious education concerns, Tom was careful to restrict his communication with her to matters of article postings for the religious education area on the site. All other matters he directed to the parish secretary.

Five months into the year, Tatum wrote Tom an e-mail informing him that, because her computer was overtaxed with the volunteer website work, she would be using his religious education office and computer to do it. When Tom checked with her, the parish secretary knew nothing of the plan. So, Tom informed Tatum that the office and computer were restricted to religious education, even if part-time, and that she needed to talk through whatever administrative equipment and space accommodations she needed with the parish secretary and the pastor, not with him.

Two days later, Tatum wrote Tom back and explained that she had spoken with the pastor. He had decided that the matter was to be settled between Tatum and Tom. If the RE office and computer could not be used for her work, the pastor told Tatum, then she was free not to work on the RE section of the web site.

This word from Tatum clarified for Tom that the pastor failed to understand the website's value or process, to comprehend the distinction between administrative and ministry matters, or to recognize the critical difference between a staff member's expectations and rights, and those of a parish volunteer. What surprised Tom, though, was that the pastor had so completely given away his own staff's power while failing to consult with them about the significance of the matters at hand.

A SECOND CASE IN POINT

Mr. Taylor Dennehy was pastoral associate for education/principal of a 257-student parish school ministry in a city neighborhood. One Thursday during lunch, a student reported lipstick writing on the boys' bathroom mirror. When Mr. Dennehy checked it out, the writing threatened the use of a gun. He immediately informed the city police, left a message on the pastor's answering machine, talked with the middle school faculty about restricting student activity for the afternoon, and began investigative work that narrowed the writing down to a small group of eighth-grade boys. When the pastor called at 2:30, Mr. Dennehy informed him that the police had not come, the boys would not name names and the teachers were restless. In fact, the pastor had already been alerted by another staff member that one teacher, critical of Mr. Dennehy's patient and non-shaming disciplinary style, was sowing discord among some teachers. The pastor could also tell by his voice on the phone that Mr. Dennhy was emotionally exhausted and administratively discombobulated. He asked if he might help.

The pastor immediately went to Mr. Dennehy's office and outlined for him a plan for the rest of the day: a letter to all parents explaining the incident and what was done to handle it, an approach to the eighth-grade boys through their parents, a brief end-of-the-day faculty meeting for information sharing and preparation for the morning, a straight-talk boundary setting conversation with the vexatious teacher, and a parent-led search process for middle school student entry into the building the following morning to offer assurances to the parent community in the event the culprit was not yet named. Freely admitting his being beside himself, Mr. Dennehy agreed to the plan and plunged into it. The pastor crafted the parent letter for Mr. Dennehy's signature, then left him to follow through on the plan, with occasional phone calls to check in.

In the weeks afterwards, the culprit caught, the teachers calmed, the parent community satisfied, and the non-supportive teacher's wings clipped, Mr. Dennehy received kudos far and wide for his handling of the situation. Taylor Dennehy was deeply grateful for the pastor's attentive intervention and hearty support when things might have foundered. For his part, the pastor felt deeply content that, in the breach, he had helped preserve Mr. Dennehy's power.

For the sake of the common good of the parish, pastors remain appropriately concerned about the distribution and preservation of power. Truly collegial pastors will distribute their power for the good of the whole community of faith and all its parts, doing so with a respectful eye to preserving, on occasion, the good of the colleagues with whom they share leadership.

» Pastoring: It's All About Trust

Pastor and councils together, in collegial relationship and in an overarching way, establish the vision for the parish, its general policies and the parish's direction. They do this oversight ministry through the processes of discernment and pastoral planning, empowered by the pastor's trusting in their judgment, their ability to keep confidence, and their trust in the Holy Spirit's work in groups. In a collegial relationship, the pastor and staff join together to implement the parish's gospel ministries in accord with the vision of them shaped by the councils.

If the pastor can let go of the mindset of Lone Ranger and Herr Pastor and embrace that of maestro and coach, then he is poised to serve the parish in full continuity with the best of the tradition and with a mindset that will work well in our age. If the pastor can let go of a self-image as bulwark of the parish and its field marshal, embracing the simple reality that the pastor is just passing through and is strongest as a generalist, then the pastor will expand pastoral leadership widely in the parish community. If the pastor refuses to be possessive of parish governance but is inclusive and trusting, stepping back from trying to control parish ministry and joining in as a colleague, then the pastor will serve hospitably and effectively as overseer, equipper, and enabler for the parish's pastoral leadership and the parish as a whole. Above all else, the pastor will mirror trust to the councils, staff, and the parish community: trust in them and trust in the Holy Spirit's work in groups.

The collegial ministry of the pastor and councils, as well as that of the pastor and staff, honoring their respective mandate, gives concrete expression to gospel ministry as it incarnates the practical meaning of hospitality in the parish's life: honoring the equal dignity of all as well as the mutuality and interdependence we share, while celebrating our unity in love and the distinct purpose of each of us in our common ministry.

IDEA!

Procure a poster or icon of the image of the divine hospitality that speaks most deeply—or all three images: Jesus' hospitality ministry, Eucharist, the Trinity—and hang it in the room where the councils and staff meet.

— PROCESS EXERCISE —

1. How do you see the corporate board function in your parish? How is it connected to the councils?

2. What do you think of the notion that the pastoral staff members serve as co-pastors of the parish?

3. What importance would you give the ministry of administration in your understanding of parish life? Do you see it as a ministry?

4. In your mind, what is the place of trust in the basic structures of your parish?

CHAPTER 6

Council Pastoral Leadership

» The High Value of Participation

The key to building trust in the parish community is the pastor's acknowledgment and promotion of the lay faithful's proper role in the church's mission (Can. 529). The pastor's making it a priority to order the parish's ministries—the essence of hospitality—flows out from Eucharist and mirrors it. If, as the second Vatican Council says in *The Constitution on the Sacred Liturgy* (CSL), "the full and active participation by all the people is the aim to be considered before all else, for it is the primary and indispensable source from which the faithful are to derive the true Christian spirit" (CSL 14), then this principle applies no less to parish life than it does to Eucharist. If with regard to the sacred liturgy pastors "should energetically set about achieving [full and active participation] through the requisite pedagogy," then the integrity of the church's life requires that pastors be similarly energetic in achieving full and active participation in parish life as a whole. This includes promoting the consultative role that parishioners properly fill in parish governance, which is integral to the effectiveness of the parish's administration ministry.

Parishioner leadership groups are the place where the pastor and parishioners (or a pastoral staff member and parishioners in the case of commissions and committees) work together to build parish-wide consensus on the parish's vision and direction, and then focus, guide, and monitor its implementation. In these leadership groups, parishioners assume their proper pastoral leadership responsibility relative to the parish's gospel ministry in collegial relationship with the pastor. Parishioner leadership groups, which are technically advisory in nature, formally take shape on three levels, each of which holds differing but related responsibilities: councils, commissions, and committees. This chapter and the two that follow will reflect on what this experience looks like in practice.

In Liturgy and Leadership

...the full and active participation by all the people is the aim to be considered before all else, for it is the primary and indispensable source from which the faithful are to derive the true Christian spirit.

» **CONSTITUTION ON THE SACRED LITURGY,**
NUMBER 14

» The Trustees

Often the pastor selects the two trustees who constitute the legal corporation, along with the bishop, vicar general, and pastor. Typically the trustees serve a specified term, for example, two years. Because of the significant weight of responsibility they bear as part of the parish's corporation, the trustees a pastor selects need to represent the parish's very best: deep knowledge of the parish, personal integrity, clear thinking, and firm commitment. The trustees are the pastor's innermost circle, the parishioners most completely informed about the parish's legal, financial, real estate, and personnel concerns. The finest trustees are completely trustworthy, unfailingly sound in their judgments, and guarantee continuity from pastor to pastor.

The nature of the trustees' place in the parish's structure calls the pastor to make a habit of informing them way up front about everything the pastor knows regarding the "soft underbelly" of parish life: pending legal action, projected estate gifts, major benefactor relationships, pending property income or expenses, potential employment difficulties, touchy Chancery concerns, and so forth. If they are well selected, they can provide the pastor with enormous support in his ministry. If poorly selected, their formal term of office allows for their passage.

A CASE IN POINT

Fr. Florian is pastor of Our Lady on the Hill. As the story about him in chapter 2 explained, Fr. Florian's predecessor, a diocesan vicar general, never fully let go of being pastor of OLH and worked energetically to block a renovation project at the Chancery. The trustees, however, had a deep knowledge of Fr. Florian's predecessor and a strong relationship. At the point of stalemate, a meeting between the vicar general and the trustees cleared the way toward forward movement when a meeting with Fr. Florian could never have accomplished it.

A SECOND CASE IN POINT

When a trustee resigned because of ill health, Fr. Francis asked a lifelong parishioner and local business owner to be trustee. In their meetings together, the trustee consistently pushed his point of view that the school was more important than all other parish ministries and, under a thin veneer of seeming to offer support, consistently criticized Fr. Francis' business acumen. Though he often felt shamed by the trustee, Fr. Francis continued to meet with him regularly, kept him informed, remained patient and kind in their exchanges, and benefited from the trustee's business advice. When the trustee's two-year term was completed, however, Fr. Francis let the trustee know that his services were appreciated, but two years was probably long enough for him to serve. It was time to give someone else a chance. However either man may have felt internally, the transition occurred without public or private rancor.

Trustees serve an enormously important function from a legal point of view. Practically, the trustees need to be kept close-in on all confidential matters, and they should be selected precisely because they are qualified to assist in these matters. By way of courtesy, the trustees should also be kept abreast of all major parish developments prior to the councils, staff, or parish being informed of them. For if the pastor should disappear from the parish scene in a crush of steel and glass on his way from the airport, the trustees ought to be so capable and well informed that the parish can pick up every issue on its plate immediately and without a hitch. The pastor's complete transparency to well-chosen trustees offers that assurance.

» The Pastoral Council

The parish's pastoral council focuses its activities around pastoral ministry planning and discerning the proper direction pastoral leadership or the parish ought to take to fulfill the church's mission and its own. These overarching charges demand practically that the council spend its time either in following a particular planning process or discerning, with the Spirit's help, what direction pastoral leadership ought to take in any given instance. The parish community's wise vision keeper with a broad mandate, the pastoral council engages itself always in the leadership tasks of planning and discernment.

THE COUNCIL'S FIRST TASK: PASTORAL PLANNING

"Where there is no vision, the people perish," says one translation of Proverbs 29:18. President Bill Clinton used this quote in his inaugural address to chide his predecessor, President George H. W. Bush, for his dismissal of what he called "the vision thing." The quotation was also a way to assert that the Clinton administration would be different. We citizens of the United States have seen a nation founder because its leaders lack vision. I have seen diocese and parish founder and wither because of lack of vision. Vision wakes people up, rouses their enthusiasm, and focuses their energy into forward movement. The effective pastoral leader offers the people vision. Vision requires planning.

Fourteen years as a pastor and ten as a university administrator have taught me that planning is the backbone of every effective organization. Planning gives contour and thrust to an organization's action. When a leader fails to offer vision, planning groups that strive to reach consensus about an organization's identity, image, characteristics, and direction can go a very long way toward supplying vision and building consensus in an organization. Coordinated pastoral planning across all parish leadership groups, then, is vital to the ongoing life of a parish community.

The pastoral council serves as the parish's planning group. Its charge is "the vision thing," and that mandate is the steel spine that holds the pastoral council process together. Planning is the top priority for a council and the engine for all its meetings throughout the year. If other matters intervene, which they always do, the planning process pauses in order to accommodate them. Approving the yearly budget, discussing the rising crisis, debriefing the bishop's pastoral visit, sorting through the pastor's latest personnel quandary, and processing how to handle the most recent absurd rumor continually interrupt the flow of the planning process. Nonetheless, planning is the task that holds everything together for the pastoral council. The implications of that for a council are enormous.

The Pastoral Council

» advises the pastor regarding the focus, guidance, and monitoring of the parish's ministries
» oversees pastoral planning
» offers recommendations on any matter that would be brought before the corporate board
» advises the pastor on all matters brought before it

An effective council process demands a good planning process (see Appendix 2 on page 244 for an excellent option).

Whatever might be selected, the planning process needs to be clear, complete, carefully articulated, easy to follow, and promising for the results the council seeks. A poor planning process leaves in its wake a rather chunky stew, both in people's minds and on paper, and neither staff nor parishioners will be able to grab hold of it or use it. The process that works will be the process that outlines explicit tasks for particular persons and groups to accomplish at precise time intervals with specified results. Nothing less is worth the council's time and effort.

Effective planning demands effective chairing of the process. It is absolutely necessary that the most competent meeting chair lead the planning process. It might also be chaired best by someone other than the person who chairs regular meetings. Split chairing can keep separate meeting tasks well focused while providing relief for both the respective chairs and the council as a whole.

An effective process includes accurate and complete recording of the group members' contributions and the reworking of the meeting material into an accessible form. This secretarial service may best be provided by the chair of the planning process. It might also be provided by the pastor from the parish's administrative staff. The less homework council members have, and the less pressure, the more interested they will be in serving the parish well during the meetings.

Writing a good five-year plan will take the pastoral council a year and a half or more. This time frame is quite normal. A highly participative process, including the gathering of accurate data, focus group discussions, and ministry commission input requires generous time if it is to be a consensus-building process for both pastoral leadership and the parish. The process is far more important than the document when it comes to planning.

After the plan is published, a monitoring process for the plan will demand extensive council involvement with pastoral staff and ministry commissions and committees. Major parish projects outside of the plan may arise which may require plan revision. A new planning process will also need to begin as the old plan schedule runs out.

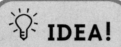

IDEA!

Keep the parish leadership groups and the whole community engaged in the common vision. Do a parish five-year pastoral plan.

- Select a planning format for the parish
- Set the total planning process for three years
- Give the pastoral council a one-year head start
- In year two implement the planning across all the ministries
- Invite focus group participation for input and feedback at major stages
- After plan completion, revisit and adjust it yearly
- As year five progresses start the whole process over again

The cycle of planning never ends, nor should it. Pastoral planning is the backbone of the pastoral council process, its first responsibility as wise vision keeper for the parish, and its ongoing task as the consensus-building engine for community.

THE COUNCIL'S MODE OF DECISION MAKING: DISCERNMENT

Day-to-day hospitality always demands from us a kind of sorting: Whom shall we invite? When? What shall we serve? How shall we serve it? What are the seating arrangements? What are the relational consequences of this event for host and for guest? If we desire to remain faithful to Jesus' revelation offered us throughout his ministry, in Eucharist and within the life of our Triune God, then divine hospitality summons us to sorting—discernment—as a way of life. That is why the Desert Fathers understood discretion to be the first monastic virtue (John Cassian, *Conferences*, "Second Conference of Abbot Moses"), why Thomas Aquinas saw prudence as the first of the moral virtues (*Summa Theologica*, Part I of the Second Part, Q. 66, Art. 3), and why Ignatius of Loyola coached the director so very carefully about the varying rules for discernment in his thirty-day retreat (*The Spiritual Exercises*, Numbers 313-336). Divine hospitality calls us to spend our days sorting out what the selfless service of extending freedom, security, and the fulfillment of others' needs looks like practically across our life.

For example, as I watched my parents age in recent years, I came to understand that if anything happened that left them diminished and unduly burdened, then I probably would need to help. Spouse, children, employment, and real estate keep my brother and stepbrother planted hundreds of miles away from my folks. While my own commitments as a diocesan priest are not meager, still I had the potential for some flexibility. So, in my communion at table with the Trinity, I weighed for some years the question of whose freedom, whose security, and the fulfillment of whose need am I best able and best suited to serve at this time of my life? I remained a happy Midwestern pastor.

My mother had a cerebral hemorrhage May 1, 2007. While at their Colorado ranch in the aftermath, I observed and reflected on my folks' freedom, security, and need. I saw their diminishment and increased dependency. I remembered watching family members care for the generation before. I reflected on the whole sweep of my life, especially in light of my having left home forty years before. I pondered, too, parish and diocesan resources, leadership and possibilities, as well as what might best serve the parish and the diocese in the short- and long-run.

While keeping the Colorado household going during those May days, it became clear to me at table with the Trinity that sharing divine hospitality, extending the Trinity's freedom, security, and fulfillment in selfless service to those who truly need it, at this time in my life probably required me not to be a pastor, but to move to Colorado to care for my folks. My bishop's generous and spontaneous permission and a new bishop's warm welcome were resounding affirmations of the rightness of the decision. Within four months of moving from Minnesota to Colorado, I was not only helping my folks, but also preaching and presiding each weekend, overseeing the local parish cluster's transition to whole parish catechesis, and writing this book.

Discernment is the essential mode of the pastoral council's operation, because hospitality in parish community life is never simply a given; questions large and small dog it. All parishes face daily decisions that demand they look at what self-emptying service and right order in relationships ought to be in this or that situation. While communities sometimes sort black from white in their effort to be hospitable in ministry, they often fumble through myriad shades of gray, and sometimes simply plunge into unknown mystery. Discernment can be tough and it is often surprising; still it is our way of life with God.

WHAT DOES GOD WANT OF US?

The first and most fundamental question in discernment decision making is: What does God wants of us? Discernment seeks God's will for parish leadership and for the community. All parish decision making, therefore, in every instance comes down to this question, which the pastor must keep ever before the council's mind and in its members' hearts. The pastor does this because it underlines the reality that the parish belongs to God and to the church, not to the council; the parish's vision and direction belong to the whole community, not to the council; council decision making is grounded in prayer, not pastor-pleasing, whim, the best bargain, parishioner polls, people pleasing, or even educated guesswork. The council's work is nothing less than sorting through the gifts and demands of the parish community's relationship with God.

CAN I LIVE WITH IT?

Discernment decision making aims at unanimous decisions. Unanimity offers the best hope, practically and before God, of the rightness of the decision. Setting the bar at unanimity places a second question for the participants in the discernment process: Can I live with this decision? That is the practical baseline for discernment decision making. Not "Do I like it?" Not "Do I want it?" Rather, "Can I live with it?"

That is also a realistic baseline because if a person cannot live with a decision being made by the group, that fact raises fundamental questions about the advisability of the decision. God lives deep within each human person, somewhere underneath our emotions and even below our experience of what we call "the gut." If at that level a person cannot live with a decision, then the discernment process needs to plunge deeper and deeper into the sorting process until unanimity is achieved.

Some argue that unanimity need not be the consensus standard. Eighty percent or above, they argue, is adequate for consensus. I don't buy it. I suggest no one buy it. If "What does God want of us?" is at the heart of what is essentially a spiritual process and "Can I live with it?" is the practical baseline-before-God question for the participants, achieving unanimity is highly likely. Over thirty years, within six ministry settings in the Great Lakes region, the Upper Midwest, and the West, I have witnessed no exceptions. Unanimity is achievable.

THE GROUP PUBLICLY STANDS BY A CONSENSUS DECISION

When a consensus decision is achieved, especially in crucial matters, the chair or pastor needs to ask every member of the council to speak out loud his or her agreement. If they have reservations, voicing them can be most helpful for the group. The "feel of the conversation," head nods, or even a show of hands are not enough to establish council consensus. Why?

A CASE IN POINT

Fr. Roger laid before the administrative council a delicate, touchy matter that was highly controversial. After lengthy discussion, he summarized the agreement he sensed in the discussion, then surveyed the room. Nodding heads confirmed a recommendation and Fr. Roger went with it. When this issue arose publicly in a parish meeting, and with some heat, Fr. Roger told the assembly that the council had unanimously agreed with the position he took. A trustee stood up and publicly disagreed. Whatever the pastor thought he might have achieved through the nodding of heads, that did not constitute unanimous consensus in the trustee's mind. Though he said nothing in the meeting or to Fr. Roger afterward, he disagreed and had not nodded. This event undercut trust in Fr. Roger and halted the momentum of his pastorate.

Once a decision is made everyone on the council, including the pastor, must stand with it publicly for the sake of the common good. In crucial matters, each member of the leadership group needs to speak his or her decision.

WHEN THE GOING GETS TOUGH

Though most questions lead readily to unanimous decisions if they are adequately discussed, unanimity is not a given. Discernment decision making can be enormously painful, as the St. Thomas College story in chapter 3 testifies. Some decisions cut so close to the baseline identity of a people or persons in the group that they challenge even the notion of discernment decision making. From the beginning the council needs to be made aware that a formal, spiritually based back-up decision-making process is available to them, and it needs to know what that process looks like (see Appendix 3 on page 251 for such a process).

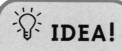

IDEA!

Use the spirituality-based consensus process once or twice as a trial run to help focus the discernment process as a whole, clarify its elements, and prepare for the times when the group gets stuck.

The formal discernment process begins with a highly discriminating and very careful statement of the question. Unanimity about the question itself begins the process of taking the group down the path of consensus decision making. Next, list the cons, then the pros. The cons are listed first because they tend to get lost. Go around and around the room to the group's satisfaction, letting each person

Discernment Decision Making

- » Focus the issue clearly
- » List the cons
- » List the pros
- » Seek areas of common agreement
- » Reflect and pray
- » Decide
- » Watch for exterior and interior confirmation of the decision

speak until cons and pros are exhausted. Then open the discussion wide to seek areas of common agreement. Oftentimes seeing common agreement awakens insight and breaks down barriers. Then break for reflection and prayer. The intensity of the process requires the break. Reflection and prayer ground the process. Following that, come back and seek further insights and common agreement. Then break for reflection and prayer again.

This double process of building tension then releasing it, bringing the group into focused discussion with each other then leaving them alone with God to sort through their thoughts and feelings, frees the participants to open themselves deep within their own minds, hearts, and souls, and open to God who abides there. Eventually this process will lead to further agreement, then a decision. Just like the papal conclave rules, extending the process until its completion serves it well. If that's simply not possible, continuing it at the next meeting should bring it to conclusion.

Once the decision is made, however, the process is not over. As time passes, the council needs to attend to factors within themselves and within the group that might militate against the decision. It also needs to attend to external factors that might preclude it: insufficient funds, the death of the pastor, etc. The making of a decision is not its confirmation; a decision's confirmation comes afterward. The council needs to remain alert to that confirmation or lack of it, and adjust accordingly.

» The Administrative Council

The parish's administrative council focuses its activities around parish infrastructure, planning and discerning its proper direction so the parish will remain secure legally and financially in the present and for the future. In practical terms, these overarching responsibilities demand that the council spend its time monitoring financial giving and income/expense trends, planning the short- and long-term budget and maintenance schedule, and discerning, with the Spirit's help, what direction parish development ought to take. The parish community's wise vision keeper with regard to its infrastructure and security, the administrative council, like the pastoral council, engages itself in planning or discernment.

THE COUNCIL'S TASKS AND DECISION MAKING

Planning is the backbone of the parish's administrative council as well. Because this council's planning attends to money and property, its process is less shaped by a formal structure like a long-range planning process than it is by the council's tasks: writing or at least approving the yearly financial report, constructing the yearly stewardship appeal, pulling together the yearly budget, reviewing monthly and quarterly financial statements, responding to the periodic building maintenance surprises, determining the yearly endowment distribution, and constructing the upcoming capital campaign. Sometimes regularly and sometimes in fits and starts, task governs administrative council planning.

Administrative council decision making relies on the same discernment process as the pastoral council, and is governed by the same two questions. The nature of its concerns, however, leads to a more informal decision-making process. Money discussions can be quite intense, but may require no major decisions. Maintenance surprises can lead to review

The Administrative Council

» advises the pastor regarding the focus, guidance, and monitoring of the parish's administration ministries

» oversees planning for the yearly budget, Sunday stewardship, the endowment, property management, and development

» offers recommendations on any matter that would be brought before the corporate board

» advises the pastor on all personnel and law matters brought before it

and hand-wringing, as well as censure, but the fix generally solves it and the payment amount is often non-negotiable. Fuzzy financial reporting can glaze the participants' eyes or elicit brisk questioning, but typically requires tweaking, not direction. Development work—the stewardship witness talk, the home visits asking for the capital campaign gift, grant writing and discussions about how to garner revenue streams beyond Sunday stewardship and tuition—is often off-loaded because council members typically demur. Fiscal long-range planning into a second year is tentative business; planning beyond three years is just short of a waste of time. The budget approval process, building facilities, or setting a capital campaign in place demands the most discernment work for an administrative council, but only the budget is a yearly, frequent-meeting process.

The technical focus of the council's planning and the expertise it requires, and the natural informality of the decision-making process save for rare instances, give the administrative council's practical functioning its unique contour.

THE ADMINISTRATIVE COUNCIL'S PRACTICAL FUNCTIONING

The pastoral and administrative councils are complementary leadership groups that depend on one another in their functioning. The administrative council, usually tempted to go it alone based only on numbers, constructs the budget in accord with the pastoral council's priorities. Its money and property recommendations, though most often accepted as they are by the pastoral council, may go forward only with the pastoral council's approval. At the same time, the pastoral council will often shrug its shoulders over concerns that have oppressed the administrative council. Yet, just as often the pastoral council will rely heavily on the administrative council's recommendations and accept them without a blink.

The effective functioning of the councils together, then, rests on three principles. Because its charge is planning and ministries, the pastoral council is the "last say" governance body for the parish on all matters, even budget. Because of the technical expertise and deep research that administrative council recommendations require, its consensus recommendations ought to be accepted as they are by the pastoral council unless it absolutely cannot live with a decision. Third, when a serious issue risks or causes disagreement between the councils, wisdom suggests bringing them together to discern the way forward.

Principles for Effective Two-Council Function

» The pastoral council is the parish's ultimate decision-making body

» Administrative council recommendations deserve consummate respect

» In times of disagreement, bring the councils together for decision making

---

In its practical functioning, the administrative council intuitively feels like a highly technical subcommittee of the pastoral council. Peace holds sway, however, when every care is taken to bring the councils into respectful agreement with one another as peers.

» The Place of Confidentiality

Complete information exchange, thorough discussion, clear advice, and balanced decision making require council members to keep confidence with the pastor and one another. Confidentiality offers the pastor the opportunity to share information at length and in depth so the councils can make sound, equitable recommendations. Confidentiality offers the council members the assurance that what they say will not be bandied about or judged in the parish community at large, and it frees the council's process to be deep and wide-ranging. Lack of confidentiality boxes a council out of some decisions, inhibits its making fully reasonable decisions, undercuts trust, and diminishes the council's and the pastor's all-around effectiveness.

CONFIDENTIALITY VERSUS SECRECY

Confidentiality differs from secrecy. Secrets are about information in the moral realm. Secrets are never part of council decisions. Confidential information, however, is part of most every council meeting.

Confidentiality means holding specified information within a particular and designated network of persons (the council) for the sake of the common good of persons in the group or groups of persons. The aim of the council's decision-making process is the common good. Therefore, the common good often demands that some issues be kept confidential (typically matters of personnel, law, finances, and some relationship issues) in the decision-making process. Keeping a matter confidential means that council members share confidential council matters with no one. This standard must be able to be met by any council member.

Confidentiality Versus Secrecy

Secrecy is the withholding of information from others, and usually implies with it the withholding of matters in the moral realm.

Confidentiality is the withholding of information within a particular and designated network of persons for the sake of the common good of persons in the group, groups of persons, or the organization as a whole.

The one exception for sharing confidences might be the council member's spouse. Couples have different expectations of one another in this area; whatever their expectations, they ought to be respected. Consequently, if a member shares confidential council information with a spouse, then spouses, too, must keep the same confidence as the council member. If a spouse breaks confidence, the council member is responsible. The breaking of council confidences, whether by the council member or a spouse, may require that the council member be asked to leave the council.

CLEARLY LABEL CONFIDENTIAL MATERIAL

Keeping confidence requires that the pastor name clearly on the agenda and in the meeting any matters that are executive session, that is, matters to be kept confidential. Ordinarily the issues to be kept confidential for the sake of the common good of the parish are as follows: matters pertaining to persons and their relationships, parish benefactor information, all personnel salary matters, matters of personnel discipline and termination, matters of hiring, parish legal matters, the particular meeting exchanges of pastoral leadership members, and the meeting discussion of controversial matters not yet decided (budget, etc.). A parish's charitable concern for people and just concern about matters of personnel, law, finances, and property offer wonderful prisms through which a pastor might consider which information ought to be shared and which ought to be kept confidential.

In fourteen years of being a pastor I never knew a council member to break a confidence. The risk of sharing more information and asking for confidentiality is well worth taking because of the enormous benefits full information brings to decision making, and because keeping information confidential is a mutually hospitable act that builds trust massively.

» Council Member Expectations

Clear expectations make good council members. That clarity demands that eligibility requirements for council membership be made clear.

The ministry described above requires that a council member be a registered parishioner willing to support the current council processes. Further, a prospective council member needs to make a three-year commitment of one and one-half hours per week, every other week, for ten months per year. Because of the way holidays and holy days fall in the calendar, the practical commitment is for eighteen meetings over ten months, summers off. Continuity in decision-making discussions, leaving room on the agenda for the surprise concerns that inevitably interrupt planning, keeping well informed about parish life, and growing in mutual relationship enough to feel comfort and trust in the group—all these factors demand semi-monthly meetings for council leadership. Meetings once a month or less frequently slow planning momentum, curb participation in real decision making, compromise full

Council Membership Eligibility

» Participation in Sunday Eucharist
» Understanding that the council belongs to the pastor
» Registered parishioner
» Support of the current council processes
» A three-year commitment
» Faithful attendance at a maximum of two 1½ hour meetings per month for 10 months
» Participation in discussion
» Commitment to prayerful discernment about the parish's future
» Ability to keep confidences

information exchange, and hobble the trust-building in relationships that makes council members truly pastoral leaders for the parish. One who would serve on the council also needs to be willing to participate in discussion, prayerfully discern the parish's future, and keep confidences.

The bottom-line expectation for council membership also needs to be crisply clear. The councils, pastoral and administrative, belong to the pastor. They are the pastor's consultative bodies and advisory groups. In collegial relationship, the council is the pastor's sounding board, guidelines establisher, idea sorter, and vision forger. The councils have no status whatsoever on their own, nor do the council members. Their immeasurable value rests in their collegial ministry with the pastor.

— PROCESS QUESTIONS —

1. What is the mission of your parish's pastoral council? its administrative council?

2. What is your parish process for future planning, and who is involved in doing the planning?

3. What do you make of the idea that parish governance is a spiritually-based activity?

4. What are your parish's expectations for council members?

5. What do you think of the notion that the councils function not on their own, but rather belong to the pastor?

CHAPTER 7

Lay Ecclesial Leadership at Work

» Background Notes

The pastor's ministry is richly complemented by that of nearly 30,000 paid lay ecclesial ministers working 20 hours or more per week in three-quarters of the parishes across the United States. Thousands more volunteer their valuable time for gospel ministry. One parish of 900 registered households, for example, calculated the yearly volunteer ministry of its parishioners at 37,000 hours. This enormous flowering of ministry in our country, a rising phenomenon since the mid-1960s, sustains gospel ministry across our national faith communities and institutions during a time when priests and religious are aging and their numbers are dwindling. While we hear often about the priest shortage, the church in the United States has no ministry shortage thanks to the competent, gracious, and selfless service of lay ecclesial ministers—paid and volunteer—in parishes, schools, colleges, universities, hospitals, clinics, publishing houses, consultation teams, and diocesan offices from coast to coast. They offer the church far more than we could ever ask for or even imagine.

Lay ecclesial ministry among priests and brilliantly capable peers can be daunting. With rare exception, lay ecclesial ministers serve in a directly subordinate role to priests. In the best settings the relationships are collegial; in the worst they are tense. Personal and professional questions, as well as culture-clash, abound between priests and lay ecclesial ministers. Nationally, that will likely remain. Given understandable institutional inclinations, few lay ecclesial ministers will ever have the opportunity to administer a parish; if they do, their tenure is likely to be brief and their service carefully monitored. Whatever the lay ecclesial minister's service, the parish setting is especially consuming, requiring many hours a week more than the employment letter indicates. Furthermore, if the lay ecclesial minister remains committed to high quality service, which the vast majority do, their ministry demands a deep, broad, and personally costly investment in people, parishioners, and colleagues, for their sake, the community's sake, and the gospel's.

Consequently, careful and sensitive reflection about what a healthy and balanced lay ecclesial ministry looks like in a parish setting is needed if relationships on every level are to be genuinely hospitable and free. Therefore, this chapter will consider staff division of responsibility and the relationship structures that support it both within staff and in the parish as a whole. Chapter 9 will consider the technicalities of employment relationships.

» The Pastoral Staff

The pastor is a ministry generalist who oversees, enables, and monitors all parish ministry service. The pastor strives to build consensus around the parish's vision and support the other pastoral leaders of the parish so they are set free to do their ministry. In a collegial relationship with the pastor, the pastoral staff oversees and resources the implementation of gospel ministry, supervises other ministers, and sets and monitors a budget area. But what does this mean day to day?

CO-PASTORS OF THE PARISH

The members of the pastoral staff are co-pastors of the parish. This term *co-pastor*—a bold term that raises hackles in chanceries and curial offices, but an accurate one nonetheless—points to a double level of collegial relationship with the pastor: individual and group.

Individual Collegial Relationship

On the individual level, the pastoral staff member, in a collegial relationship with the pastor, holds broad discretionary oversight responsibility over the ministry areas in his or her portfolio, including everything from the particular ministry's vision to the specifics of its implementation. The parish hires a pastoral staff member to exercise precisely this kind of responsibility.

The pastoral staff member complements the pastor's generalist stance in relationship to the parish by approaching the parish's life through the prism of his or her particular ministry. This particular ministry approach not only nuances, but also helps to give fuller shape to the whole of the parish's ministry. The pastoral associate for worship, for instance, views the parish from the angle of the enormous treasury of the liturgical and musical tradition of the church, and invites the pastor, fellow staff members, and the whole parish to be mindful of that perspective as a way of stretching their understanding of the parish and its ministry. The pastoral associate for lifelong learning does the same from the perspective of the church's catechetical tradition, even as the pastoral associate for business affairs and the pastoral associate for education/principal do the same from their perspectives.

The history and culture of the parish, the pastor, colleagues, the parishioners, and the council-established vision for the parish all have their effect on the pastoral associate's ministry-focused stance, and they shape the contribution he or she makes to parish life. At the same time, however, the contribution the pastoral associate makes to the parish and pastoral leadership from the perspective of his or her background, education, and particular ministry portfolio provides wonderful color, texture, breadth, and depth to everything the parish plans and does.

The Pastoral Staff as a College

Each pastoral associate is a member of a little college called the pastoral staff, which gathers regularly with the pastor. The pastoral staff—pastor and pastoral associates together in collegial relationship—form "the pastoring ministry" of the parish. Just as the local church is truly complete only when the full assembly—priests, deacons, religious, and the whole people of God—gathers with the bishop around the table of the Lord for Eucharist, so the pastoring ministry of the parish is complete only in the context of the pastoral staff group, which represents the full complement of the parish's gospel ministries.

That is to say, none of the pastoral staff members alone represents the fullness of the parish's pastoring ministry. Rather, each represents an aspect or element of it in accord with his or her ministry portfolio. Even the pastor, though a generalist, represents essentially the presidential ministry of the parish. The pastor does not represent the fullness, for example, of the parish's worship or religious education ministry, nor does the pastor represent the totality of the parish's ministries. A parishioner's questions about religious education classes or choir membership, for instance, require the pastor to forward them

to a pastoral associate. The whole pastoral staff gathered together as a group, however, expresses the fullness of "pastor"
and "gospel ministry" for the parish community.

Consequently, the pastoral staff's role for the community of
faith is to reflect together regularly on the whole parish's gospel ministry. This reflection takes place in a very full ecclesial
context: the ministry guidelines promulgated by the universal,
national, and local churches, the limits and possibilities articulated by the pastor, the vision set by the pastoral council, the allocation of resources established by the administrative council,
and the sensibilities developed by the ministry commissions
(see below). Nonetheless, pastoring the parish, in general and
from every angle, is the collegial purpose of the pastoral staff,
with the pastor presiding over the college's ministry.

The Overarching Purpose of the Pastoral Staff

Pastoring the parish, in general and from
every angle, is the collegial mission of the
pastoral staff, with the pastor presiding.

THE THREE-MEETINGS SET

Implementation of this vision requires three levels of meetings. The first is a one-to-one meeting, the other two are group
meetings. The effective pastoral associate will conscientiously
participate in each and strive to make them as constructive,
forthright, thorough, and forward-looking as possible. On the
first two levels, so will the effective pastor. These meetings for

the pastoral associate are with the pastor one-to-one, with the pastoral staff as a group and with the ministry area's parishioner-staffed commission.

The Meeting with the Pastor

Whether they are full-time or part-time, paid or volunteer, and whatever the blend of their ministry responsibilities, the pastoral associates and pastor need a regular, one-to-one meeting together. This meeting aims to develop common expectations for ministry, clarify performance concerns, offer perspective on performance weaknesses, elicit reasons for falling short of expectations, open up planning possibilities, and generally deepen the relationship between the pastor and pastoral associate. So long as this meeting is a give-and-take process between the pastor and pastoral associate, it will help develop competencies, clarify expectations, strengthen bonds, and build trust. The meeting can also be a great deal of fun as the pastor and pastoral associate explore mutually interesting theological issues, practical concerns, and pastoral approaches to individuals and groups.

While formal individual meetings need to occur at least twice per year for supervisory purposes, informal, casual meetings circulating about the parish center and popping into one another's office help to build rapport among pastor and staff. While the frequency and formality of the meeting might be determined by the size of the parish more than by any other single factor, as a rule of thumb the pastor and pastoral associate holding an individual meeting every other week should be more than adequate.

The Pastoral Staff Group Meeting

The group meeting has a different purpose. It aims to tie-back and tie-across basic information about each of the ministries and the parish as a whole, to help the pastoral associates and

Staff Members

» Meet regularly in a group setting with their functional peers and only occasionally with other staff members
» Seek personal support and friendship outside the parish, not in it
» Set aside their disagreements and dislikes so they can work well together as professionals

pastor together clarify a common vision for the parish, to encourage the members of the group to become increasingly collaborative in their ministry together, to share resources, and to build relationship in the group. Because the experience of these meetings varies widely from parish to parish, several comments may help set some outside boundaries in their regard.

A CASE IN POINT

When St. Lawrence the Martyr holds its staff meeting everyone comes: the pastor, pastoral staff, secretaries, maintenance supervisor, and sometimes the kitchen coordinator. While this sort of meeting may be useful occasionally for sharing general information, it inhibits pastoral staff discussion and planning for gospel ministry, and engages them in secondary and distracting concerns. It also pulls administrative staff into pastoral staff concerns, which can be confusing and even disruptive for the meeting, staff relationships, and parish ministry. The pastoral staff holds the gospel ministry portfolio. Other staff groups exercise different responsibilities. Each group needs to be honored in its own sphere, but with separate meetings so that effective, focused ministry might move forward.

A SECOND CASE IN POINT

When St. Simeon the Stylite holds its staff meeting, things tend to bog down into the pastoral staff members' personal concerns with one another and social activity planning. Because staff members seek the satisfaction of their personal needs within their professional relationships, hidden agendas occasionally create rumblings that keep them from constructive parish ministry business. Planning trips to the local amusement park and lunches out distract the staff from its focus as well. Gospel ministry requires focus. While an occasional luncheon or outing can have its place, that place is not merely secondary, but tertiary to staff meetings. Staff members also need to be encouraged to seek personal counseling and friendship outside the workplace.

The Pastoral Staff Meeting Purpose

One-to-one:

» Develop common expectations
» Clarify performance prospects
» Get perspective on and reasons for weaknesses
» Open up planning possibilities
» Build and deepen relationship

Whole group:

» Tie-back and tie-across basic information
» Build a common vision
» Encourage collaboration
» Share resources
» Build and deepen relationship

A THIRD CASE IN POINT

The staff members at St. Olaf the Warrior King dislike each other. Ideological divergence, turf battles, and personality differences keep staff meetings and the office environment tense. This circumstance requires strong and creative leadership that calls staff members to a professionalism that rises above disagreements and disaffections so the staff can plan gospel ministry and collaborate together to do it. It may call as well for occasional blunt talk at a staff meeting to set boundaries. An incisive pastor may even see that the situation requires staff change as the only remedy.

The pastor and pastoral associates benefit greatly in their ministry together if they do the very hard work to help cohere the pastoral staff in their ministry as professionals, ministers, and co-pastors sharing in the oversight of the whole parish and its gospel ministry life.

The Ministry Commission

Each gospel ministry of the parish, or blend of them under the oversight of a pastoral associate, requires a parishioner commission. Pastoral staff members come and go—the parishioners are the stable parish community, so it is a high priority that parishioners participate in focusing, directing, and monitoring each of the parish's gospel ministries, just as they do in council for the ministry of the parish as a whole. Ministry commissions offer continuity in gospel ministry, help keep it organically centered in parishioner experience, and widen the parishioners' knowledge base about gospel ministry. While commission members need education to be effective in the leadership group's mission, they offer an irreplaceable complement to the pastoral associate because of the depth and breadth of their experience of and access to fellow parishioners day to day. Commissions also spread ministry knowledge and experience widely in the parish, enriching parish life. Commission membership is a major formational tool for every parish. Not least of all, the commission helps nurture the bonds of community among the parishioners, even as they nurture pastoral leadership.

The Commission's Function

The ministry commission's mission is to focus, guide, and monitor a particular gospel ministry area in a collaborative relationship with the pastoral associate. The function of the ministry commission in relationship with the pastoral associate parallels that of the pastoral council in relationship with the pastor. That is, the ministry commission assists with planning for the gospel ministry area, offers recommendations on any ministry direction concerns that would be brought before the pastoral council, re-

The Ministry Commission

» advises the pastoral associate regarding the focus, guidance and monitoring of the pastoral associate's ministry area

» assists with planning for the ministry area

» offers recommendations on major ministry direction concerns that would be brought before the pastoral council

» reviews the ministry area budget before it goes to the administrative council

» advises the pastoral associate on all matters brought before it

» establishes *ad hoc* committees to help with its work if necessary

views the ministry area budget before it goes to the administrative council, and advises the pastoral associate on all matters he or she brings before it. In given instances, if necessary, the commission establishes *ad hoc* committees to assist it with its work.

Planning for a particular ministry area is the backbone of the commission's work. Effective planning by a commission, however, requires that the pastoral associate educate the commission members about the ministry area: its purpose and history; the universal, national, and local church guidelines that govern its mission; the various pastoral considerations that determine this or that course of action; its financial demands on and benefit to the parish; and its relationship to the other gospel ministries. The pastoral associate's very first priority needs to be thoroughly equipping the commission members for their ministry so they will offer effective pastoral leadership. This education and formation will look different for each ministry area.

Commission decision making in a particular ministry area relies on the same discernment process as the councils, and is therefore governed by the same two questions: What does God want of us? Can I live with this decision? Spirituality grounds the process, and a formal, spiritually based discernment process backs up the commission's effort to achieve unanimity in its decisions (see Appendix 3 on page 251).

Structuring Commissions

The structuring of a ministry commission's task requires careful attention. The commission's responsibility should be the large picture: the ministry's general contours in the parish, ministry area policy, and particular issues that the pastoral associate finds it helpful to discuss with the commission. The day-to-day details of the gospel ministry area should be left to the pastoral associate.

A CASE IN POINT

Isaiah Pope, the pastoral associate for worship, established a liturgy commission at St. Cajetan's. It took four meetings for the parishioners to tell their personal stories and get acquainted with their basic responsibilities, two meetings for Isaiah to offer a basic overview of the church's liturgy and introduce the commission members to the liturgical books, and ten meetings for Isaiah and the commission members to read and reflect together on the topics that fundamentally educated its members for the commission's work: the church, the sacraments, other liturgical rites, and pastoral liturgy. For example, it was important to learn why to celebrate the Liturgy of the Hours instead of a communion service on

Parishioner-staffed Ministry Commissions

» educate parishioners about the basics of gospel ministry
» honor parishioners' rightful place in focusing, guiding, and monitoring the parish's ministries
» place parishioners at every level of ministry planning and discernment
» offer continuity and insight within and across the parish's gospel ministries
» build parish community life
» center the pastoral associates in real parishioner experience of ministry
» prepare parishioners to serve in parish and diocesan governance structures

weekdays, why bring the body for the funeral rather than cremated remains, and why we insist on witnessing marriages in church instead of on the beach. This first year of education readied the commission members ably so that over the next two years, they could help Isaiah shape a pastoral liturgy that belonged to St. Cajetan's, formulate policy in the liturgy area, evaluate liturgical celebrations and seasons, and equip incoming commission members—all the while minimizing the commission's temptation to micromanage (which every pastoral leadership group will do if given the chance). If a commission can be effectively structured for liturgy, it can and must be effectively structured for any ministry area.

Leadership Group Designations

COUNCIL: a group called together for consultation, discussion, and advice

COMMISSION: a group called together to perform specified duties

COMMITTEE: a group appointed to consider, investigate or report on matters of a certain kind. This task-oriented group is always and only *ad hoc*.

BOARD: a group of persons who gather to manage or control an entity in an ongoing way. Parishes have no boards but the corporate board.

The ministry commission structure in the parish educates parishioners about the basics of gospel ministry, helps them join with pastoral staff in building a common direction for each ministry in accord with the parish's council-established vision, honors the parishioners' rightful place in sharing the hosting and being guest in the parish, and builds parish community life. The ministry commission structure also centers the pastoral associate in parish members' experience of the parish's ministry, which helps the pastoral associate to shape truly pastoral ministry for the parish. The ministry commission is an indispensable tool for the deep evangelization of the people that our age requires.

The Pastoral Associate's Meetings

The set of three meetings in which the pastoral associate participates all focus, direct, or guide the pastoral associate's ministry in the parish. They also offer the pastoral associate abundant opportunity to shape the ministry of the pastor, colleagues, parishioners, and the parish as a whole. Effective participation in these pastoral leadership structures extends the pastoral associate's hospitable care to the parish community as a host, even as it graces the pastoral associate as a guest of the parish community and its pastoral leadership.

» Relationships with Administrative Staff

The administrative staff, in a collaborative relationship with the pastor and pastoral staff, provides ongoing support for the gospel ministries of the parish mainly in the areas of communications, finances, property management, and record keeping. In larger parish settings, administrative staff members also serve in a complementary, collegial relationship with a pastoral associate in his or her particular area of ministry.

Unless multiple people perform the same function, administrative staff collaboration best occurs in individual rather than in large group meetings. The emphasis of a pastor's or pastoral associate's meeting with administrative staff would be developing common expectations, clarifying performance concerns, problem solving, and general deepening of relationship. Formal interviews between an administrative staff member and his or her supervisor need to occur twice per year, but informal, casual meetings usually fill the bill day to day.

At the same time, pastoral and administrative staff collaboration requires regular and clear communication. Informing the receptionist about the coming guest or announcing him, preparing useful and timely information for the bulletin and website, learning how much money is left in the budget and how much to budget for next year, adhering faithfully to the room reservation procedures, forwarding the baptismal certificates for recording—all of these tasks, and far more, require close collaboration between pastoral and administrative staff members. Occasionally procedure establishment and policy change involves an administrative staff member in a pastoral staff meeting, or vice versa. This collaboration is natural and necessary, and needs to be kept as simple and straightforward as possible.

Staff performance concerns, should they arise, ought always to be raised with the staff member him- or herself first, and only afterward with the staff person's immediate supervisor, if that seems necessary. Conversation among fellow staff members about such matters is inappropriate. Social gatherings among all staff—celebrating the monthly birthdays, for instance—can be great fun and help to build relaxed, congenial relationships, at least as long as the gatherings remain all-inclusive.

» Parish and Leadership Variations

LARGE STAFF AND SMALL STAFF CONSIDERATIONS

The megaparish (1200 registered households and above) will often have several staff members in a gospel ministry area: a pastoral associate for religious formation, a staff member for adult formation and another for youth ministry. Staff members entrusted with ministry service in collegial relationship with and accountable to a pastoral associate are something of a cross between pastoral and administrative staff. In general, staff relationships in a single or blended area of gospel ministry should be treated like the relationship between pastor and pastoral staff, with the pastoral associate functioning with his or her staff like the pastor might with the pastoral staff. Position titles might be more like that of the administrative staff as well, for example, Director for Adult Ed or Youth Director. The pastor and pastoral associates together might decide how to handle who comes to what meetings. Consistent practices will assure comfort for all.

The family parish will often have four staff members: pastor, secretary, part-time religious formation person and part-time bookkeeper. By way of stereotype, the secretary usually holds enormous power in this situation simply because that is a full-time position and its holder is present in the office; no one else is. This situation, too, requires flexibility. Ought there be a formal group staff meeting? Is communication adequate without it? Again, mutually agreeable consistency will assure relative comfort for all.

CLUSTERED PARISH CONSIDERATIONS

Clustered parishes present a touchy challenge for any pastor because they are usually a mix of smaller and large communities, with some sites closer and others farther apart, that remain consistently sensitive to their differences, prerogatives and favoritism of any sort. Clustered situations can be highly complex. The pastoral staff structure options for such a circumstance—country or city—are essentially three: a centralized, a blended, or an extension model.

The centralized model assumes that one site, either the largest or most centrally located, will function like a "cathedral parish" for the whole cluster. This model would suggest establishing a single set of gospel ministry-connected pastoral associates who would oversee particular ministry areas at all sites, with other staff members hired to help, depending on parish resources.

The blended model assumes the distinct identity of each site and strives to honor that while, at the same time, it works to make gospel ministry coherent across the cluster. This model would establish a single set of site-connected pastoral associates who would minister with the pastor, the people at each site and other staff members hired to help, depending on cluster resources. The site-connected pastoral associates would coordinate the gospel ministry at each site.

The extension model assumes distinct site identity while making little effort to cohere the communities. This model would bless whatever is and work with it, largely relying on volunteer ministers at each site and administrative staff members functioning for the cluster. This model might have only a pastor and secretary full-time, with a part-time religious education coordinator and part-time bookkeeper. It may or may not rely on blended councils, depending on site proximity, population, and finances.

Each of these models has strengths and weaknesses. Many clusters find themselves in the process of evolving from one model to the other, or moving back and forth, because of staff and resource shifts. The real situation of clusters, of course, is less tidy than the models.

The important point is that, as a general rule, a strong ministry team needs to work collegially with the pastor if parish pastoral leadership is to build and keep trust. This bias favors either the centralized or the blended model, and would require that the pastor minister with a strong blended council if the extension model is to mirror genuinely hospitable and effective pastoral leadership.

» In Summary

Across parishes in the United States, tens of thousands of lay ecclesial ministers sustain gospel ministry. These dedicated men and women, often in awkward circumstances, make an enormous and indispensable contribution to the ministry life of our church. Their effectiveness rests in their collegial relationships with the pastor, their colleagues, and the parishioners as they collaborate together in parish gospel ministry commissions. The careful structuring of both the pastoral and administrative staffs in the parish, a structuring that respects their differences yet honors their interdependence and complementary functions, expresses and mirrors to all a most gracious hospitality.

— PROCESS EXERCISE —

1. How effectively do the three contexts of meetings—one-to-one with the pastor, with the pastor in the pastoral staff group, and with the ministry commission—work in your parish for stimulating participation and bringing about effective ministry?

2. List the contributions the ministry of your parish administrative staff makes to the parish.

3. What difference does the size and shape of your parish make to the model of ministry offered above? What would work? What wouldn't?

CHAPTER 8

The Third Table of Parish Life

» The Meeting: Conduit for the Spirit's Work

Fr. Maur took for granted the high value of the pastoral leadership meeting. To him it was the womb for the parish's vision and the boiler room for its life; it organized the organization. So, when he inherited a 1,400 family Midwest parish, he sought the pastoral council's consensus about meeting purpose, schedule, and mechanics, and then implemented it.

Seven meetings along, Fr. Maur sensed a change in the council, an energy and verve that he thought new, so he took aside a council member and asked about it. She told Fr. Maur that his predecessor had used the council meetings to plan welcome events for newcomers; that's it. "We're feeling a little windburned in these meetings, Father," she shared, "but it is exhilarating to have our opinions respected and to be doing so much—and we're all talking about it!"

Six years later, after an especially difficult discussion that finally reached a consensus conclusion, a trustee, who in various capacities had been part of meetings during Fr. Maur's tenure and his predecessor's, quipped with a wink, "How I long for the days when we only planned parties for newcomers!"

How often do we hear, "I hate meetings!" Whenever I have probed the remark, invariably this caveat emerges: "Well, I hate meetings where we spin our wheels and go on and on. But if there's something we need to talk about and do, and the meeting stays on task and moves along, then a meeting's OK." Though that response remains less than full-hearted, it none-theless captures what needs to be a critical concern for pastoral leaders: successful meetings.

THE CHURCH'S LIFE: FED AT THREE TABLES

Our celebration of the Eucharist is the source and summit of our life as a community of faith. Our breaking open the Scrip-tures at the table of God's word, our eating and drinking the Body and Blood of the Risen Lord around the table of the Eu-charist—the two-table Eucharistic event breaks us open to the breath of the Holy Spirit's life and the fire of the Spirit's power within and among us as a people. Our action around the table of the word and the table of the Eucharist feeds us as a people of faith, drawing us further, deeper, and ever more meaningfully and vulnerably into communion with God and one another.

The ambo and altar are noble pieces of furniture located prominently in the church, at the parish's very heart. They are tall tables, thirty-nine inches tall, elegantly fashioned for au-gust purpose. But there is a third table where we are fed in par-ish life. It is a common table compared to the altar and ambo, and measures only sixteen or seventeen inches in height. This low table is the one around which parish leadership gathers. Compared to the table of the word and the table of the Body and Blood of the Risen Lord, the pastoral leadership table is a humble and homey one. It is set for snacks, beverages, and napkins. It holds extra agendas, pens, and working papers. I have seen a foot there, too, on occasion. Though it is less prominent and far more humble than the other two tables of parish life, nonetheless the low table around which pastoral leadership gathers is vital to parish life.

If pastoral leadership is essentially a group experience, and if effective pastoral leaders gather in groups to exercise leadership animated by the Spirit's life and power, then the table around which pastoral leadership gathers, though it is a low and humble table, also feeds the parish's gospel ministry life, drawing us further, deeper, and ever more meaningfully and vulnerably into communion with God and one another. The low table of pastoral leadership, along with the table of the word and the table of the Eucharist, is the place where heaven and earth meet in parish life.

THE THIRD TABLE, A LOW TABLE

The third table of parish life is a low table because it serves two purposes. The first is gracious hospitality and the second is reflective discussion.

The aim of the pastoral leadership meeting is to build consensus around the parish's vision and many of that vision's particulars. This purpose requires deep personal engagement and the free flow of ideas because it focuses on meaning: the meaning of gospel ministry, the meaning of parish life, the meaning of church, and the meaning of the Holy Spirit's life and power among us manifest in the Spirit's gifts. This purpose also requires vulnerability. The first question that governs the ministry of a pastoral leadership group—What does God want of us?—calls pastoral leaders to open to the divine life among them and within the parish community. They need to risk engagement with one another and be forthright about their ideas and perceptions. The second question that governs pastoral leadership decision making—What can I live with?—calls group members to open to the divine life within. They need to risk self-knowledge and honesty about it. The low table serves both meaning and vulnerability.

The high table barricades group members against both. It calls people into what is on the table rather than into each other; it tells them that they have work to do, work outside themselves. The high table under fluorescent light is a field for a joust: reviewing reports, critiquing programs, planning events, hammering out details, and horse trading. The high table, in spite of the physical closeness of those around it, allows people to fold their arms across their chest, pull back, rock on the chair's hind legs and hide. The high table may be necessary for pastoral leadership meetings on occasion, when the entire agenda concerns papers that are piled high for review. Nonetheless, the pastoral leadership group should avoid the high table for its meetings.

Why is this issue important? Physical space creates an atmosphere that tells participants a group's purpose and a meeting's aim. A low table in soft light—plates of cookies, coffee mugs, milk glasses, and napkins in the center—invites people to graciousness. It tells them that the meeting is about them, what they think and feel. The atmosphere relaxes the group, conveys warm regard for the people assembled, and implicitly honors them as persons whose discussion and opinions are highly valued. In this environment, as opposed to the high table, group members offer their best thinking, gradually feel comfortable enough to offer emotional responses, and, over time, develop warm enough relationships to engage one another deeply. These dispositions are exactly what the pastoral leadership group meeting requires.

If you look again at the book cover, you will note that the Trinity sits around a low table, gathered at a cup of wine. If you recall your culinary history, you will remember that Jesus reclined at a low table whenever he joined in a reconciling meal with anyone, including the Last Supper. These are the models for the third table, the pastoral leadership table, in the parish and across the whole church.

» At the Table: Content and Process

Focused on meaning and open in vulnerability, pastoral leaders gathered around the third table of parish life serve as a conduit for the Holy Spirit's work in the parish. Therefore, two complementary elements must be strong-

Seven Guidelines Regarding Meeting Content

The chair...

» calls the group members to make the real decisions that focus, guide, and monitor the parish and its ministry life

» gives the group everything it needs to make good decisions

» trusts the group with confidential material

» keeps the decision-making process spiritually grounded

» participates as an equal in the consensus decision-making process

» publicly honors the group's decisions

» remains short-run and long-run accountable to the group for its decisions

ly, solidly in place for the meeting: stout content and effective process.

STOUT MEETING CONTENT

Seven rules of thumb govern pastoral leadership group content. First, the chair invites the group members to make real decisions that focus, guide, and monitor the parish and its ministry life. Parish and ministries planning, the hiring of staff members, sudden reduction in staff force, the school ministry's proposed tuition scenarios, staff salary raise proposals, the rectory budget, the renovation of the offices, the stewardship appeal theme and presenters, the clash with the neighboring property owner about the parking lot—all large, real, directional items for the parish need to be brought to the pastoral leadership group for review and decision.

Second, the chair gives the group everything it needs to make good decisions. Information sharing makes or breaks decision making. Objective details, unvarnished and without slant, provide a parish leadership group with the grist for well-informed and balanced decision making. When in doubt, share the information. Third, careful decision making requires that the chair trust the group with confidential material. If the group knows only some details, it can make only partial recommendations. Full decisions require full disclosure, full transparency.

Fourth, the chair keeps the decision-making process spiritually grounded. What does God want of us? That is the umbrella question for all group considerations. Before God, what can I live with?—that is the bottom line for each member of the group personally.

Fifth, the chair participates as an equal in the consensus process. This demands the chair's frankness about his or her perception of what God wants and what is personally livable. The chair seeks meaning along with the members of the group, and needs to be every bit as vulnerable in the decision making as the rest of the group. The chair's participation as an equal forges strong, sustainable decisions.

Sixth, the chair publicly honors the group's decisions and, finally, remains accountable for them to the group short- and long-term. The proof of trust rests in the follow-up (guideline seven). If the decision is right and good, it needs to be followed to the letter. If upon further consideration it is questionable, it needs to be brought back to the group for review.

What if leadership ignores the decision and goes its own way? Every year Fr. Tom hosted a once-over-lightly budget meeting with the administrative council. He always agreed with the council's recommendations in the meeting. Every year, immediately after the meeting, he gathered with one of the trustees and the business administrator. They ordered cheeseburgers from a local tavern, poured themselves a scotch and did the budget Fr. Tom wanted. When leadership ignores group decisions like this, it undercuts trust, its own leadership, and the Holy Spirit's work, and it inevitably collapses into all sorts of lies.

Robust meeting content builds trust within leadership, and among leaders and the people. It also makes for robust pastoral leadership and parish life.

EFFECTIVE MEETING PROCESS

Meeting process, however, is equally important. The pastoral leadership meeting is not about merely human business, but about God's business. On every level—staff, councils, commissions, committees—its aim is to serve as a conduit for the Spirit's gifts. So, what do effective meetings look like in their process? Carefully structured meeting rules establish the boundaries for respect in the group. Astute meeting leadership keeps participants engaged and tasks focused. Artful meeting mechanics keep the process moving efficiently. A meeting grounded in prayer helps keep the pastoral leadership group open to the Spirit's gifts.

Ten Rules for Meeting Conduct

Effective group process requires that the leader, or the group as a whole, establish rules to shape expectations. Group rules presented, discussed, and agreed upon at the very inception of a group's work make for good order and set a common standard for measuring what being out of order looks like. Rules offer guidelines for respect and courtesy in a group. The rule setting need not be elaborate, but it ought to be clear and pointed. Ten basic rules govern all pastoral leadership groups

First, when group members cannot make it to a meeting, they should communicate that to the chair or a designated group member. Pastoral leadership is a commitment. The chair needs to convey to group members that their attendance is valued and important. If someone cannot make a meeting, he or she ought to be accountable enough to e-mail or call a designee so the group will not waste time wondering and waiting at the meeting's start.

Second, participants need to come on time. If a meeting starts promptly, the group can begin business and accomplish more. As a rule of thumb all meetings start seven to ten minutes late—in the U.S. Midwest and West at least. The chair ought not to grouse, but to plan for that. Still, getting the meeting going as close to on time as possible will help get the participants there and ready to begin.

Third, all group members need to participate fully and forthrightly in the meeting process. The parish needs the best thinking of everyone in the group if it is to serve the parish well. As a rule of thumb, if it's on one person's mind it's on others' minds, so there's no need to be shy about speaking one's point of view. When participants speak up, question ideas, disagree, and hash things out, they are engaging in fertile meeting discussion and assuring that the meeting's outcome will belong to the whole group. Everyone needs to speak and be heard in a group's process.

At the same time, group members must honor what other participants offer. Marguerite was eighty-four and said yes to membership on the parish's worship commission. No matter how much she was coaxed, Marguerite had little to say. But when the time came for the commission to host the appreciation dessert party for the liturgical ministers, Marguerite led the planning, acted as hostess for the event, and supervised clean-up. The pastoral leadership group always honors the participation its members offer.

Group members often develop gritty attitudes toward certain subjects or one another. Fifth, they therefore must be encouraged to "bat the camel on the nose." If one participant is having trouble with another, then he or she ought to deal with the trouble forthrightly and kindly outside the group. If a group member sees bothersome patterns arising within the group, then he or she needs to ask the group to talk about them, and the group needs to honor the request. Batting the camel on the nose prevents the whole smelly camel from getting into the tent.

The Prophet Muhammad says that all our words must pass through three gates. The first gate is truth. All our words must be true. The second gate is necessity. All our words must be necessary. The third gate is kindness. All our words must be kind. Sixth, all group participants do well to remember Muhammad's three gates.

Seventh, group participants need to pray: What is it that God wants of us? Pastoral leadership groups are about the great work of gospel ministry. *Robert's Rules of Order* and majority-rule reduce decision making to maneuvering for power; they should be banned from every pastoral leadership group table in the country. The pastoral leadership group aims to build consensus in the whole parish around what God wants. If group members have a personal agenda, and most do, then they need to be forthright about that or drop it. If the group knows personal agendas up front, that filters remarks, nurtures patience, and saves time. If a group member drops it, everyone is set free. The essential question that matters around the table is always a prayerful: What is it that God wants of us?

Eighth, group participants need to ponder: what can I live with? The group's process is essentially spiritual and intended toward unanimity. Its decisions are not about politics, though politics will be considered from time to time. If someone cannot live with a decision, the group needs to thrash that out, talk it out, pray it out. That's what the fallback consensus process is for (see Appendix 3 on page 251). The question before a pastoral leadership group is never: Do I like it? Am I excited about it? The question, given what God wants of us, is always: Can I live with it?

Ninth, confidentiality expectations require careful review. The ability to share confidential material allows group members to speak their minds freely and securely, enables the group to make well-informed decisions and permits the group to take the time it needs to decide a matter without interference. If the group cannot keep confidentiality, then trust is undercut and the group's place in decision making will be marginalized. Confidential matters need to be designated as such, and group members need to understand that if they break confidentiality they forfeit their right to sit at the table. For the sake of the common good, confidentiality must command high respect from every group member.

Finally, all pastoral leadership groups need to publicly support consensus decisions. In meetings people can argue points of view and even wrangle so long as they remember Muhammad's three gates. But when group members leave the room, they need to stand by the consensus achieved and be able to explain it with clarity and enthusiasm. When group members leave a meeting they are not partisans but ambassadors. The parish community deserves that from pastoral leadership groups. If a group member plays the partisan about a consensus decision, he or she risks being sidelined by the group.

Ten Rules for Meeting Conduct

1. Come on time; if you cannot attend, please let someone know
2. Participate fully and forthrightly
3. Accept courteously the participation level other group members offer
4. Listen
5. Remember everyone else's contributions are as valuable as yours
6. Remember Muhammad's three gates
7. Pray: what does God want of us?
8. Think: what can I live with?
9. Respect confidentiality
10. Be publicly supportive of the decisions we make

A CASE IN POINT

Eddie was a trustee who disagreed with Fr. Derrick's handling of a property concern with a parish neighbor. Eddie raised his disapproval in the parish rather than with Fr. Derrick. The reaction of Eddie's fellow administrative council members was to withhold their opinions when Eddie was in the room, and to hold back from Eddie personally outside the meetings. Fr. Derrick still received their frank opinions, but outside the group and accompanied by hand-wringing about Eddie. Within six months Eddie got the message and resigned.

The ten simple rules discussed here (and see box on page 135) set boundaries for graciously courteous group interaction. At the very beginning of their process, all leadership groups need to reflect on common expectations and set out their rules for engagement. All groups need occasional reminders, too. Rules are also vital for dealing with the difficult participant.

A SECOND CASE IN POINT

Fr. Placid, a new pastor, watched quietly as the school board completed a smoke-and-mirrors budget. Afterwards the principal came to him and protested, "If we go down next year, and we will with this budget, it will hurt us irreparably. We've got to redo it."

Over the next two days they did. Fr. Placid then called an executive session school board meeting to present the redone budget. During the discussion the board reached consensus around a modified budget, except for one person, who indicated publicly he wanted to speak with another parishioner before he made a decision. He was clearly threatening to break executive session confidentiality. He maintained that position even when that was pointed out to him by the group.

Since consensus was blocked and breach of confidentiality was threatened, Fr. Placid told the board that he and the principal would decide the school's budget and inform the board at a convenient time later. Afterward, he took the board member aside and told him—to his wide-eyed amazement—that if he broke confidentiality, he would forfeit his seat on the board. Fr. Placid ultimately kept the whole situation calm by implementing the redone budget the board was ready to approve, but clear group rules are what allowed Fr. Placid to move as he did to preserve the common good.

Pastoral leadership groups generally run smoothly when they establish common expectations that respectfully honor the group, its participants, and the common good of the parish community. Lack of rules undermines good order, and it risks chaos and hurting people.

THE EQUAL VALUE OF PROCESS AND CONTENT

While a limping meeting process can still accomplish something if the meeting's content is steak and potatoes decision making, that decision making will nonetheless suffer from incompleteness, confusion, and lack of follow-through because of the limp. On the other hand, brilliant meeting process fails the parish and the Holy Spirit if meeting content is but parsley and maraschino cherries, delectable as they might seem for a fleeting moment. The ideal is to bring both elements together: real ministry decision making with an effective, efficient, spiritually based process, the combination of which results in channeling the Spirit's gifts by expressing what God wants from the parish for the sake of its gospel ministry.

» The Meeting Chair: Astute and Gracious Listener

Competent meeting chairing requires skill. Some would argue it is an art. It is, in fact, an acquired skill that becomes art in a master's hands. The meeting chair makes or breaks meeting effectiveness and the good experience of the participants. Two questions about meeting chairmanship deserve particular reflection: Who chairs? What does effective chairing look like?

WHO CHAIRS THE MEETING?

In an ecclesial setting, the chair for a meeting ought to be the person to whom the meeting "belongs." For the pastoral or administrative council, the right meeting chair is the pastor because the councils are consultative and advisory to the pastor. The same is true for the pastoral staff meeting. The collegial relationships of the pastoral staff pivot on the pastor, therefore the meeting belongs to the pastor and the pastor ought to chair it. The natural chair of the ministry commission meeting is the pastoral associate because the commission is consultative and advisory to the pastoral associate. The selection of a chair other than the pastor or pastoral associate in these instances risks distorting the meeting and setting up the chair for failure.

A CASE IN POINT

Like the parish pastoral council for the pastor, the diocesan presbyteral council belongs to the bishop. When John R. Roach was Archbishop of St. Paul and Minneapolis, I had occasion to attend council meetings. The presbyters of the Archdiocese always elected an "executive director" for the council (the Archbishop remained technically "the president") whose primary task was to chair council meetings. The meeting's physical arrangement was high, long tables set in a very large, open-centered square. The chair of the meeting always sat at the middle of one side of the square. Archbishop Roach always sat at the middle of the opposite side of the square, facing the chair. The Archbishop was widely respected as a formidable administrator, well known to be brisk about business, and he was nothing if not a straight shooter. I watched many an executive director sweat profusely as he tried to manage an unwieldy and outspoken crowd through a jammed agenda with the Archbishop's every move controlling him—often unwittingly, sometimes directly—from across the room. It was painful to observe, but no doubt far less painful than sitting in the executive director's chair.

In the church, groups "belong" to certain functionaries. To step outside that structure for the meeting chair risks the substitute chair's being manipulated or publicly shamed. Clean lines of authority and responsibility demand that group leadership follow the natural lines of authority and responsibility if at all possible.

That said, the first principle of meeting chairmanship is that the responsibility for chairing a meeting ought to rest with the person who best runs a meeting. If the pastor or pastoral associate cannot lead a meeting capably, the value of a well-run meeting is higher than that of any particular person leading it…if the person to whom the meeting belongs will honor that leadership.

Rotating chairmanship is ill-advised and majority ballot elected chairmanship is a not-at-all-worth-it shake-of-the-dice. Consequently, since fill-in chairmanship for an ill-suited pastor or pastoral associate ought to rest with the person in the group who is most competent, that qualification may need

Principles Regarding Meeting Chairmanship

» The person best able to function in the role chairs a meeting

» If capable, the person to whom a meeting "belongs" best chairs a meeting

» All meeting participants accord the chair their attention, cooperation, and respect, including the person to whom the meeting "belongs" if he or she does not chair it

to be discerned and it may take some time and testing to do that. Neither inclusivity nor popularity, however, warrant derailing effectively run pastoral leadership group meetings. The most capable ought to chair meetings.

In the end, whoever leads the meeting, this principle also applies: everyone participating in the meeting needs to accord the chair attention, cooperation, and full respect, neither usurping the chair's authority nor undermining it. That includes the non-chairing pastor or pastoral associate.

THE COMPETENT CHAIR

The skills for conducting group process boil down to three constellations of qualities: attentive listening, the ability to integrate ideas, and respect for the participants.

Attentive Listening

God gave us humans two ears and only one mouth. Good meetings begin and end with accepting God's gifts in accord with God's priorities.

The effective meeting chair works hard to accurately understand each participant's contribution. Good listening demands that the chair summarize contributions carefully, and help contributors and the group sort through to the precise idea a participant is attempting to communicate. If the chair keeps the subject matter clear for the group—the conversation's context, focus, and content—then the effort to unpack participant ideas and lay them before the group will carry the meeting forward and bear much fruit. Listening in writing assists the chair enormously in the effort to summarize what has been said. Writing contributions down on newsprint or a blackboard allows the group to revisit ideas and most graciously affirms the contributor.

Integrating Ideas

The work to integrate ideas requires that the chair offer idea organization options and ask provocative questions, thereby helping the group to connect ideas, expand them, and think through their implications. Integrating ideas also requires that the chair let go of his or her own ideas, detaching from personal points of view, even those dearly held, for the sake of serving the group. The effective chair dies to his or her own perspectives so the group's mind and heart might rise in the meeting's process.

Respect for the Participants

The effective chair encourages everyone's participation and respects what's offered. This respect means letting a clarifying conversation run on sometimes, and at other times bringing sidebar discussions to a close. It also demands occasional handstands to help everyone around the table feel affirmed even when their contributions are "a little off." Often this affirmation is better done after the meeting instead of during it. Respect also requires the chair to bring discussion to a crisp end and summarize it so the whole group can appreciate the meeting's accomplishments. Respect for others, honoring them and their contributions, keeps meetings hospitable. Failure to respect offends people and hobbles group process.

Effective meeting chairmanship requires astute listening skills, sufficient intellectual agility and self-deprecation to integrate the group's ideas, and unyielding respect for everyone participating. These skill constellations comfort meeting participants and build trust in the chair.

The "Astute and Gracious Listener" Meeting Chair

Listens well...
  » accurately summarizing
  » helping the group sort
  » clarifying ideas
  » focusing ideas into context
  » writing contributions down

Integrates ideas...
  » keeping the overarching context to the fore
  » relating ideas to one another
  » offering organizational options
  » asking provocative questions
  » detaching from his or her own point of view

Respects meeting participants...
  » encouraging participation
  » honoring every participant
  » letting clarifying discussion run
  » bringing wandering discussion back to the point
  » landing the discussion at meeting's end

» Some Meeting Mechanics

ESTABLISHING THE AGENDA

The agenda for the pastoral leadership meeting comprises two parts: a fluid segment and an established segment. All meetings require this division.

The Fluid Agenda Segment

The meeting's fluid segment is a brief, meaty, information-sharing session. Information sharing ties-across and ties-back facts within the parish's ministry life. It prevents communication silos from developing within and among pastoral leadership groups. It also alerts the group to rising problems, quells rumors, eases group interaction, and serves as a meeting warm-up. The fluid meeting segment unburdens group members by easing their concerns, builds trust by filling in gaps, and frees the participants and the chair for the main business of the meeting. In the rarest of instances—rampant rumors the school is closing, a parish-wide meeting that collapsed in disaster the night before, parishioners rising up because a worship staff member has just been terminated—the fluid segment of the meeting becomes the meeting's business.

The Established Agenda Segment

The established segment comprises the meeting's major business. These agenda items are either agreed upon at the end of the previous meeting, submitted to the chair between meetings, or are set by the chair. Because the meeting belongs to the person who sets the agenda, item assembly before the meeting demands careful reflection.

If the established segment consists of items agreed upon by the group at the end of the last meeting—far the preferred method for establishing an agenda—then the work of setting the agenda consists of arranging the items in logical sequence and setting time limits for each. The chair does this work, and then sends the agenda and all supporting materials out to the participants beforehand, either by e-mail or US mail, so that meeting participants can prepare themselves for the meeting.

All agenda items are assigned a discussion time so the chair can determine what business can be accomplished and what needs to wait. This exercise forces clear prioritizing. Time allotment also structures the meeting and alerts meeting participants to the anticipated depth of item discussion. The time assignments need to remain somewhat flexible, but only minimally so. The person responsible for presenting an item—a particular member offering a report, for instance—ought to be noted on the agenda as well. Meeting participants appreciate immensely the opportunity to prepare for a meeting beforehand by seeing a structured agenda and having the opportunity to study supporting materials. This hospitable gesture tells the group that the parish wants their considered opinion.

If the agenda is assembled through participants submitting items—often the case with pastoral staff, for instance—then this process needs structure. First, a generous deadline for item submission must be established and kept. Second, the meeting chair, along with the person to whom the meeting belongs if he or she is not the chair, must review the submitted items to consider if each is worthy of group discussion. Matters better handled between two group members, asking the group to make a decision that is one person's responsibility, putting someone on the spot or calculated to irritate—such matters need to be kept off the agenda. If there are such matters, then the person to whom the meeting belongs should talk to the submitter about why the item will not appear.

A CASE IN POINT

Mary was pastoral minister. She had a habit of submitting agenda items that raised questions that should have been addressed in a brief meeting with the pastor. For over a year, whenever Mary submitted "off the mark" items, the pastor would discuss the items with her personally and then clarify why they were inappropriate for the agenda. Gradually, Mary's discussions with the pastor in one-to-one meetings became more direct and the off-the-mark agenda submissions ceased. The discussions between Mary and the pastor ultimately emerged as the primary trust builders for Mary and the pastor in their relationship; hesitancy to trust had been the unspoken reason Mary submitted the inappropriate items.

Deftly handled, the delicate task of engaging with the people who submit off-the-mark agenda items gives the person addressing the submissions a wonderful opportunity to sharpen a participant's sense of what smooth functioning of the group's decision-making process requires. The estimated time necessary to address off-base submissions also determines the submission deadline.

If the chair, or the person to whom the meeting belongs, adds items to a group-determined agenda, then he or she needs to explain at meeting start why these items are on the agenda.

Setting a proper agenda is half of any meeting's accomplishment. The importance of a well thought-out agenda, sent out to meeting participants beforehand along with its supporting documentation, cannot be underestimated. The chair also needs to remember: the group members develop a sense of the chair's openness to being accountable through their experience of the agenda assembly process. The agenda-setting process either builds trust, or undercuts it.

MEETINGS AND TIME

Effective council and commission work requires that meetings be scheduled every other week for ten months a year. Meetings once a month may be suitable for reports and the review of brief concerns, but they cannot serve for serious pastoral leadership and all that it requires. If pastoral planning is the group's task, then meeting twice per month, ten months a year, gives the group time and momentum enough to get somewhere. Honoring holiday breaks and summers, meeting every other week for ten months shakes out to about eighteen meetings a year. Given the authority and responsibility that the councils, pastoral staff, and commissions hold, participants are most willing to give meetings this amount of time.

The Meeting Agenda

PRINCIPLE: the person who sets the agenda owns the meeting.

In pastoral leadership groups, agenda items are...

» agreed upon at the end of the previous meeting,
» submitted to the chair between meetings for review and arranging
» or set by the chair

The first is by far the most hospitable method.

Regarding length, nothing worthwhile happens in a meeting beyond ninety minutes. All parish meetings should honor this guideline. Long meetings tire people, drain energy, and lead to fuzzy thinking, crankiness, manipulation, and bad decisions. All parish meetings should be planned for no longer than ninety minutes. If a meeting extension is necessary to complete an item's discussion, then group permission should be sought. If given, the extension ought to be less than fifteen minutes. Failed permission means the meeting ends on time. People deeply appreciate time-limited meetings. If the meeting starts late, honoring the end time anyway builds warm regard for the chair of any group.

Meeting agenda items are time-limited as well. Listing item time limits up front orients meeting participants to keep a meeting moving. Sometimes an item requires more time than the chair planned; that's just fine so long as the chair ends the meeting on time.

If the planned agenda is short, less than an hour, the meeting ought to be deferred or cancelled. If planned discussion falls short, going home early is a gift. If a quorum fails to show, the meeting ought never to begin.

BEGINNING, ENDING, AND IN-BETWEEN

After the meeting's information segment, the chair needs to offer the group a brief overview of all the items upcoming. This overview shows the group members the meeting's course and allows them to offer caveats on items based on unknowns or new information. The overview also gleans for the chair informal group consent to what is to come.

As the chair moves through each agenda item, he or she needs to offer a very brief contextualizing introduction. Meeting participants require constant reminders about what an agenda item means for the parish and its gospel ministry. Developing the context saves discussion time because people forget where an item comes from, how it fits, what it is connected to, why it is important, or why it needs to be discussed at this time.

Meeting wind-down needs to begin ten minutes before the projected end time. By six or five minutes before meeting end, the last three always-stable agenda items need review. First, the chair summarizes the meeting; a précis allows the group to offer clarifying and forward-moving observations that sharpen agenda planning. Second, the chair asks what will be on the agenda next time. Consent about the upcoming agenda items bolsters group participation for the next meeting, affirms the group members' value, and simplifies agenda assembly work. Finally, the chair affirms the date, time, and place of the next meeting. If meetings are scheduled in advance this task is simple, if not, it will likely require some processing time.

These niceties at the beginning of a meeting, the end, and in-between, clean up and simplify the meeting process for everyone, particularly the chair. They also develop comfortable expectations that help the group run well.

MINUTES?

Minutes ought to record only group decisions. A terse summary of reports can be helpful. Recording meeting discussion is unnecessary. A brief listing of decisions and bottom-line report results ought to accompany the next meeting's agenda when it is sent out. The parish files should attach the minutes to the meeting agenda and be done with it. Minutes are necessary for the councils, and helpful for commissions and committees. They are less relevant for the pastoral staff.

Who does the minutes? Parishioners are wary of doing minutes as they understand them. The less the participants have to do outside the meeting, the more they will enjoy and invest in the meeting. A parishioner participant recording minutes is a last option.

The ideal candidate for doing minutes is the chair. Why? The agenda is already in the chair's computer and can serve as an outline, the chair has immediate access to what was recorded during the meeting and the chair usually experiences the meeting more vividly than anyone else. This proposed form of minutes takes no longer than fifteen minutes to produce. It is time well spent for the chair.

» Meeting Prayer

Prayer opens and closes every pastoral leadership meeting. The Holy Spirit's presence and power is invoked at meeting start, and God receives the glory at meeting end. But what ought that look like?

Some parishes structure an extended reflection on the Sunday readings. Others pray briefly. Yet others invite participants to take turns offering prayer. Still others share prayer. All of these can work. Some, however, take quite a bit of time and either extend the meeting or limit work. Some can be an imposition and uncomfortable.

A brief and relatively formula-oriented prayer puts most people at ease and serves every pastoral leadership group well. The longest of these might be one of the little offices of The Liturgy of the Hours. A single psalm or a prayer from one of the many marvelous collections of them serves the purpose admirably as well. Putting people on the spot to pray can intimidate the prayer and unsettle the group. Opening the group up for spontaneous prayer can lead to grandstanding or an ill-advised "praying at" people: "That we may grow beyond our anger at the pastoral associate for religious formation; that she may change and we might ourselves open to healing, we pray to the Lord." A brief and formulaic prayer works best for pastoral leadership

Meeting Tips

Set the meeting environment to help set meeting tone

Offer light refreshments

Keep prayer formulaic and short

Let the most skilled at chairing lead the meeting

Set agenda item limits

Listen, listen, listen

Information share briefly every time

Offer the context for each item before discussing it

Limit meetings to 90 minutes

Keep listening

Get group permission to exceed time limits

Summarize the meeting's accomplishments

Discuss the agenda for next time

Agree on the next meeting's date and time

Keep brief, summary minutes

Give God the glory

groups. Done mindful of the liturgical year, this prayer form can be instructive and moving.

The meeting ought to end always with the briefest of prayers, a set formula. People are usually ready and anxious to go. This prayer time gives God praise and thanks for what has been. The doxology, "Glory be to the Father …" works extremely well. People respond instantaneously and automatically, the prayer is appropriate and the praying says, "The End."

Hurling javelins to the heavens is an ancient and venerable way to understand prayer. The image well characterizes what pastoral leadership group prayer ought to look like. Prayer invokes the Holy Spirit, gives God the glory, and plants the ministry of the group solidly in the soil of God's vineyard. Elaborate prayer risks extended meeting time and ruts in the road.

» A Final Note

Between 1962 and 1965, the world witnessed most astonishing proof that the Holy Spirit works in groups: Vatican II. Council historians write that the journey from the preparation commission work to the the final Council documents was full of amazing turns and surprises. Along with the Scriptures, our tradition and the life of the church day to day, the Council's history affirms that the Holy Spirit works in groups. All we can say in light of that truth is: Glory be to God for the third table in parish life!

— PROCESS QUESTIONS —

1. What do you think of the notion that all parish pastoral leadership groups serve as conduits for the Holy Spirit's work in the parish?

2. What is the very worst experience of a meeting you ever had? Why was it so?

3. What is the very best experience of a meeting you ever had? Why was it so?

4. What is your experience of the difference between "low table" and "high table" meetings?

5. What would you add to the "Rules for Meeting Conduct"?

6. What is your opinion about the "Principles Regarding Meeting Chairmanship"?

CHAPTER 9

Cultural Conflict: The United States Context and the Parish

» The Parish: A Living Organism

The word *parish* conjures in our minds basic assumptions about the shape of people's relationships, the structures for providing its material needs and the general contours for what people and leaders believe and think—all of which are what we mean by the word *culture*. We assume these cultural patterns on two levels. On one level, we expect our basic suppositions to take flesh in all parishes everywhere: South America, Europe, Asia, Africa, Oceania, and North America. On another level, we have enough experience to realize that each parish expresses a particular coming together of relationships, provisions, and thought patterns that mirrors its own singular history, location, people, and leadership. Every parish shares in a universal culture even as each has its own unique culture. The Maasi out on the Althi Plain of Northern Tanzania may wear blankets and beaded neck disks, gather under the oriteti tree for Eucharist, and wonderfully dance their praise and thanks, yet we expect them to stand and sit at the same ritual points, take up a collection and count it, and share fellowship after Mass. They fulfill our expectations on both levels, as do parishes across the globe.

Yet, between the universal and the unique parish culture there is a middle level. On this level, however brilliant the gift of each parish's unique cultural expression of the universal Body of Christ, cultures clash. This cultural conflict level of parish life, which also exists in all parishes, differs in the United States parish from what may be found in South American, European, Asian, African or Oceanian parishes. Because cultural conflict lies at the root of so many of the ordinary struggles of day-to-day parish life in the United States, pastoral leaders do well to consider the origin of these cultural conflicts, the points at which the clash occurs, and how the clashes might be addressed.

Church and Culture

If the blood of the church is history, the flesh of the community of Christ is culture.

» THOMAS O'MEARA, O.P.
THEOLOGY OF MINISTRY, PAGE 23

Three culture clashes will be considered in this chapter and the next. This chapter will consider cultural conflicts that emerge from our U.S. context: American governance culture versus church-based governance culture, and the conflict between the parish being Mystical Body of Christ as well as an American corporate employer. The next chapter will explore the conflict between education culture and church culture in the parish with a school ministry.

» CONFLICT ONE:
American versus Church Leadership Assumptions

Most Americans wishing to participate in governance bodies such as parish councils come to leadership with cultural biases. That is, many would assume they come to leadership as a representative of the parishioners, that the leadership group provides checks and balances on the pastor or pastoral associate, and that the leadership group in the parish assumes at least a semi-legislative function. Many also tend to presume that group members, especially at the council level, ought to be elected from the whole community by a secret, majority-rule ballot.

Many primary pastoral leaders fail to address these assumptions, and even accept some of them. From the viewpoint of a church leadership body, however, these ordinary, normal American biases are secondary, and sometimes contradictory to how pastoral leadership and ecclesial decision making work.

PASTORAL LEADERSHIP IS ABOUT COMMUNION, NOT REPRESENTATION

The cry at the time of the Boston Tea Party was "No taxation without representation." Ever since, American ideals seek representation for the people's opinion on every issue of concern to the commonweal. The American notion of representation in a leadership group includes within it the understanding that a person comes forward into leadership to stand up for a constituency so its voice can be heard. This notion presumes, therefore, a certain "us" and "them" in gathering for group decision making.

From an ecclesial point of view, however, everyone around the table shares in the one Body of Christ. All are brothers and sisters in Jesus Christ. The pastoral leadership group, then, never assembles as "us" and "them," but only as "us," all one body in Jesus Christ. The pastoral leader has no constituency; he or she represents, always, the whole body, not merely a part of it. As our tradition understands it, the pastoral leadership group is a sacrament of the whole Body of Christ held together by the sinews of our all being washed clean by baptism, nourished in Eucharist, and anointed and animated by the Holy Spirit. Pastoral leadership groups are an expression of this sacramental communion.

For this reason, the assembly of a pastoral leadership group ought to be done with an eye to its being an expression of the whole parish community, but not, strictly speaking, representative. The pastoral council comprised of representatives from parish clubs, committees, and organizations, for instance, begs for trouble in fulfilling its purpose to plan and discern for the parish as a whole. Representatives of constituencies in an American context usually give priority to the constituency, not to the common good of the whole. A representative council of this sort most often will not and cannot achieve consensus around a whole parish vision. Instead, it leans toward the endless processing of constituent concerns, disallowing the council to rise above them to plan for the whole. The sink for doing dishes that the seniors from St. Columba wanted installed in their meeting room was always far more important than any other issue the pastoral council discussed. An emphatically representative pastoral leadership group always hazards getting stuck in constituent concerns.

The Church: One in Christ

Although the universal Church of God is
constituted of distinct orders of members,
still, in spite of the many parts of its holy
body, the Church subsists as an integral
whole, just as the Apostle says: "We are all
one in Christ," nor is anyone separated from
the office of one another in such a way that
a lower group has no connection with the
head. In the unity of faith and baptism, our
community is then undivided. There is a
common dignity...

» POPE ST. LEO THE GREAT, SERMON 4

Though pastoral leaders might keep an eye on the rightful concern to represent, within reason, the whole parish around the table of its leadership groups, pastoral leadership is not essentially representative. Rather, the pastoral leadership group is an expression of the whole parish's unity, the bonds all share in communion together as one body in Christ.

PASTORAL LEADERSHIP IS ABOUT PARTICIPATION, NOT CHECKS AND BALANCES

The notion of checks and balances in governance, which leaves us Americans feeling secure in the interplay of our government institutions, presumes polarity—perhaps cooperative, perhaps adversarial—within government structures. This presumption of polarity carries with it the assumption that decision makers oversee the results of decision making.

From an ecclesial point of view, however, the pastoral leadership group gathers as one body, each person having a complementary role to play as he or she participates in a common ministry. The role of the group member is to be the whole parish's head, heart, eyes, ears, and hands in advisory or consultative counsel, and to provide expertise to help pastoral leadership discern decisions about the parish's present and future. While church governance documents make it clear that every pastoral leadership group serves a consultative function, experience makes it clear that as trust builds the pastoral leadership group effectively serves a deliberative one.

The purpose of the pastoral leadership group is to focus, guide, and monitor the parish's gospel ministry, all the members bound together in solidarity, participating together in a complementary way for the sake of the gospel mission. Leadership accountability is a high value that needs to be kept solidly in place. Still, the pastoral leadership group's purpose is neither checks and balances nor any other form of oversight, but rather common participation in the gospel mission.

PASTORAL LEADERSHIP GROUPS ARE ENGAGED IN DISCERNMENT, NOT A LEGISLATIVE PROCESS

Our American notion of the decision-making process in government is that legislators exchange wide points of view among as many as possible, then the majority comes to agreement through majority vote on what is the best course for the most. American decision-making processes presume majority rule and some horse-trading to get to it. The result of that process is law.

From an ecclesial point of view, however, the purpose of the decision-making process is to sort through to what it is that God wants of us. What God wants of us may represent a majority opinion. It may not. The very nature of the process means that all the options need to be placed on the table and considered, but the end result is a prayerful, reflective sorting through to a unanimous conclusion about what it seems God wants of us. This sorting process is messy. It includes some experimentation, some soliciting opinions, some "let's wait-and see" as the group observes the external confirmation of its decisions, or lack of it.

The majority's opinion is an important datum in ecclesial decision making, but not the aim of the process. The aim is what God wants, and the result is subject to internal and external verification (see Appendix 3 on page 251). The councils are engaged in a discernment process, not a legislative one.

PASTORAL LEADERS ARE ELECTED BY DISCERNMENT, NOT BY MAJORITY BALLOT

The ecclesial concept of election to leadership also differs from American assumptions. The American notion of election is running for office, secret ballot and majority rule. The ecclesial notion of election does not preclude American assumptions, but modifies them.

Whether the position to be elected is pope, Eastern Rite patriarch, or abbot, election rules require more than simple majority rule. The aim of election in a church setting is the largest possible agreement, effectively discerning toward consensus. Consequently, except for extenuating circumstances, two-thirds is most often required for election to an ecclesial office. In the church, people do not run for office. Instead, they are nominated, then their qualifications are discussed by the group as a whole or on the side. Ecclesial "election" is a personal and group discernment process.

In a parish setting, discernment-oriented election to a council position makes sense. Some parishes enter into an extensive process of community-wide prayer and reflection in which people are recommended or moved to come forward. Other parishes begin the process with a council discussion, then invite volunteers forward in the bulletin, tap people on the shoulder, or ask people whose name surfaces if they are interested in serving. These "elected" are then interviewed to discuss candidate interest and suitability, and clarify mutual expectations. Methods vary widely across parishes. All, however, are a form of "election."

For the sake of setting reasonably accurate expectations for a pastoral leadership group, the American style of election to the council is least suitable. It runs the very high risk of bringing people into leadership who are focused on representation rather than communion, checks and balances rather than participation, and legislation rather than discernment. These suppositions in pastoral leaders can create a terrible drag on the leadership group's process, and real conflict. Pastoral leaders are best elected by expectations-clarifying discernment, not majority rule.

BEING CLEAR ABOUT THE DIFFERENCES

Instructing prospective and current council members about the above differences between ecclesial and American leadership group assumptions allays both fears and difficulties. Because these cultural assumptions are so ingrained in us Americans, pastoral leadership groups need at least yearly reminders about the differences between U.S. and church presuppositions. This clarity can make a critical difference, especially at council election time.

A CASE IN POINT

Evelyn was widely experienced in city politics, twice running for office. She sought election to the parish's pastoral council. The pastor asked Evelyn for an interview. When they met, the pastor explained council expectations, underlining for Evelyn the difference between American and ecclesial presuppositions.

Church vs. American Leadership Assumptions

Pastoral leadership groups are about...

» communion, not representation
» participation, not checks and balances
» discernment, not legislation
» election by discernment, not election by majority vote

"You know, Father, that doesn't fit me at all," Evelyn reflected. "I don't think the council is a good idea for me." Her response relieved both of them and alleviated many an awkwardness.

The cultural conflict between American and ecclesial leadership assumptions in pastoral leadership groups dictates that everyone around the table needs to know precisely what is expected of them, and consents to the expectations. In church decision making, the pastoral leadership group's great gift is its visionary, discerning, confidentiality-honoring relationship with the chair, and the person to whom the group belongs if he or she is other than the chair. Forthright group member recruitment done with integrity, therefore, requires that pastoral leaders make clear to current and prospective leadership group members what the expectations are for their happy participation.

» CONFLICT TWO:
Body of Christ and American Corporate Employer

As a particular instance of the Mystical Body of Christ, the parish is a people and a place where heaven and earth meet in divine embrace. Its mission is to live and extend the gracious hospitality of God through gospel ministry. At the same time, however, the parish is a legal U.S. corporate entity, with all the attendant privileges and responsibilities.

From the corporate point of view, every parish is a small business. Our average U.S. parish with a school would own $12 million in property, have a cash flow in excess of $2.5 million, employ forty people, maintain 60,000 square feet of space on an acre of property and have approximately 2,400 immediate stakeholders. This corporate reality means that the community of faith is subject to myriad national and state laws and regulations. It also means that the pastor, chief executive officer of the corporation, is the official employer of everyone who works for the parish corporation, with all the privileges and responsibilities that entails.

A CASE IN POINT

Fr. Hannibal was appointed pastor of a 1,200 family parish with a school that was having serious difficulties. The school parents, up in arms over an unexpected 37 percent tuition hike for the next year, were threatening to take their children out of the school. The school ministry was overstaffed—three full-time teachers taught a Kindergarten enrollment of eighteen students—and the principal, seriously ill, had been increasingly absent from the school over the previous three years. The endowment had been depleted by 60 percent in five years.

The debt sat at $2 million. The newly hired business administrator could find no record of how much money was either owed to vendors or sat in the bank.

Fr. Hannibal huddled with the trustees and councils, and they began their stabilizing work. Three years later, school ministry enrollment had settled at one-half the previous levels, the endowment had been secured, the parish knew what it owed and held, and it was paying its bills. A parish staff of 42 had been reduced to 28, and 16 of those were newly hired. In this massive staff change, only one case of employment arbitration arose, and that ended in a split decision that parish insurance covered. All the while, of course, Fr. Hannibal presided at Eucharist, preached, baptized, married, buried, and visited the sick and the schoolchildren.

Though Fr. Hannibal's parish circumstances were highly unusual, the corporate realities of every parish are fearsome and demanding. Because of the enormous impact it has on people's lives, the deep investment parishioners and staff have in one another, and the profound justice implications of it, no element of the parish's corporate responsibilities is more imposing than employment. The ramifications of the parish's serving as an employer touch all of the parish's ministries. Consequently, every pastoral leadership group, particularly at the council and commission level, needs to understand what the parish's employment responsibilities mean for the parish and demand of it.

AN OVERARCHING NOTE
Because of its responsibility for and legal relationship with each parish within it, every diocese establishes policy that governs employer/employee relationships. So does every parish. This

policy is supposed to be articulated in a handbook available to all employees. These are corporate documents with an ecclesial subtext. They declare that the diocese/parish is either an "at will" employer who can dismiss an employee at any time, or a "just cause" employer who may dismiss an employee only after the completion of certain prescribed processes. All church entities need to be—even if not theoretically—most certainly in practice, a "just cause" employer.

THE EMPLOYMENT CONTRACT

Employment is a contractual relationship. The employee agrees to offer his or her services to the parish in exchange for financial compensation, benefits compensation, assistance for performing the assigned job well, and reasonable job security.

Ministry Descriptions

The efficient functioning of any organization depends on the clear and detailed job descriptions of its people. The job—or better, ministry—description provides grist for the mill of compensation discussion, gives the potential employee a clear sense of the position's requirements, and offers the employee and supervisor an ongoing basis for analyzing the expansion, contraction, and effectiveness of the position, the employee, and the interrelatedness of all the positions in the organization. Carefully wrought ministry descriptions are indispensable in the parish.

A CASE IN POINT

Dierdre was hired to be full-time parish secretary for the All Holy Angels Catholic Community mentioned in chapter 1. The parish's only full-time employee, she received minimal direction from the five pastors for whom she worked over eleven years.

As Fr. Joe, also mentioned in chapter 1, became Dierdre's sixth pastor, it became clear very quickly that he was disinclined to supervise Dierdre. Rather than offer her clear limits and direction, he withdrew his office to the rectory. As he did so, Dierdre began calling herself "office manager" and quit accepting direction from her formal supervisor, the business administrator, who was part-time. Having succeeded in making that shift without reprimand, Dierdre then took to calling herself "assistant to the pastor." Fr. Joe simply shrugged both moves off, as well as their implications.

At the same time, Fr. Joe allowed Dierdre to become the only doorway to the pastor; her phone line and answering machine was the parish's only access to him. With all parish calls coming to her, Dierdre began taking initiative to deal with concerns that might otherwise have come to the pastor's attention. In the process, she established wider relationships within the parish and gained fuller information about it, further enhancing the power of her position.

Fr. Joe knows well that he needs to sit down with Dierdre to review her formal and informal title acquisitions and mushrooming ministry description, and then do a ministry description with her that sets out clearly her authority and responsibility. Confident of his own power, however, and hating conflict, he demurs. Meanwhile Dierdre, defending all her moves as an effort to serve and lead in light of the pastor's lack of availability, continues to insert herself, according to her own preferences, in every area of the parish's ministry.

Clear, detailed ministry descriptions (see Appendix 4 on page 258 for two samples) focus all compensation and performance analysis discussions between a supervisor and an employee in the parish no less than in the business corporation. Because they detail all elements of a particular position, ministry descriptions, used well in hiring and for ongoing discussion, save enormous time and energy that can be wasted in all sorts of personally painful and even legally messy controversies.

The Parish Hiring Process

Pastoral leadership, particularly the pastor, needs to be especially attentive to the hiring of new staff members. Any hiring process requires valuable time and energy, and its failure drains the parish's emotional and financial coffers. Staff hiring ought to be done always by an *ad hoc* search committee, always aimed at hiring persons outside the parish and always aimed at avoiding the employment of current parish staff family members. Hiring is the point at which committee members who represent parish constituencies are most valuable.

The search committee for a pastoral associate ordinarily needs to include a trustee, a pastoral council member, another pastoral associate and parishioners who are closely familiar with and impacted by the ministry area. Occasionally a "member of the opposition" is wisely included on a pastoral associate search committee. The pastoral associate hiring committee might include seven persons.

The search committee for an administrative staff member ordinarily needs to include a pastoral associate and parishioners knowledgeable about the area of expertise for which the person is being hired, preferably members of a council or commission. The search committee for a maintenance supervisor, for instance, requires a member of the administrative council, the business administrator, the pastoral associate for education/principal if there is one, and a couple of parishioners deeply knowledgeable about maintenance. The search committee for a bookkeeper requires a similar configuration, including the trustee who is corporate treasurer. The committee for an administrative staff member is no larger than five persons.

The pastor is never a member of a search committee. The pastor may sit in on the ministry description discussion for purposes of clarification, the interviews for the final round of candidates, and the final discussion that determines recommendation ranking. The pastor may also wish to interview the final candidates for a pastoral associate position so he, the candidates, and the search committee develop a sense of "fit" with the pastor. Still, because the committee's purpose is to

Parish Hiring Rules

» A representative search committee interviews the candidates for hiring

» The pastor is never member of a search committee

» No person whom the new person will supervise is member of a search committee

» Applications are always taken from persons outside the parish

» No immediate family member of parish staff need apply

» The search committee recommends candidates in priority rank to the pastor

» The pastor hires from the submitted ranking

» If that fails, the committee's work continues

» The search committee dissolves once the pastor hires or the process, by consensus, is deferred

Guidelines for the Typical Search Committee Process

A. Application:
- Post the position opening through the diocesan network and/or local newspapers.
- Set the deadline for application three weeks later

B. Meanwhile, the search committee meets to:
- review the ministry description for glaring omissions or mistakes
- discuss and agree upon the kind of person the parish needs in the position at this time
- forge questions for the interviews

C. After deadline completion, the search committee meets to:
- review preliminary resumes to determine the candidates it wants to interview (usually no more than three)
- continue to forge questions and develop scenarios for applicant response
- establish a basic schedule for
  - » interviewing with the committee and/or other concerned persons
  - » touring facilities
  - » meeting people

D. The search committee conducts interviews, asking each candidate identical, pre-prepared questions

E. The search committee achieves consensus, recommending candidates in priority order to the pastor for hiring

F. The pastor
- hires the new staff member
- and informs the committee and the parish once documents are signed.

discern a person's objective congruence for the position and the parish, and to make priority ranked recommendations of candidates to the pastor, the pastor is never a member of a search committee.

A CASE IN POINT

In June, with the parish hall being renovated for a re-dedication and the classroom building still a mess, St. Joseph Cupertino's maintenance supervisor resigned. Desperate to get work done and pressed for time, the pastor and pastoral associate for education/principal asked a parishioner if he wanted the position. An independent jobber with fine building skills, he took the job, then asked if the parish would hire his son to help get the work done. The parish did that.

After the first ninety days of probation, the new maintenance supervisor showed himself to be a lone wolf. He resented direction, had poor supervisory skills relative to his staff, favored his son over other employees, chafed when his favoritism was pointed out to him, and began to leak his disaffection to staff members and parishioners. Subject to the formal employment disciplinary process surrounding all these matters, eight months into the job the maintenance supervisor was helped to see that he needed either to resign or be terminated. He chose to resign. The fallout in the parish, however—whisperings in corners, silent glares from the former supervisor and his family in and out of church, the withdrawing of some parishioners from congenial relationship with the pastor and principal—was painful for everyone. It was no wonder. The pastor and pastoral associate for education/principal had broken every hiring rule in the book.

Following the hiring rules and the search committee process no matter what saves pastoral leadership and the parish as a whole from immense headaches. It is never, ever worth it to succumb to the temptation to short cut the hiring process. Doing so most always backfires.

Compensation

In the past, women religious bore an enormous burden of service for little but eternal compensation. In our time, financial compensation to lay ecclesial ministers is a major commitment of parish life. With a school or without, a parish will typically invest in excess of 80 percent of its expenses in personnel. That is as it should be. Because the standard of living differs from one area of the country to the next, most dioceses have established their own standards for this compensation. While there are occasional exceptions and policies do demand close scrutiny—one diocese, for instance, honors only five years of experience when an elementary teacher transfers from one school to another no matter how many years of experience he or she has accrued, a patently unjust policy—the diocesan standards for compensation ought generally to be followed. For all of the nobility of ministry in the church, no church employee should ever be harmed by stingy compensation. Just hospitality requires that all who work for the church have their basic needs met in proper proportion to their employment commitment and common professional standards.

The high cost of health insurances makes benefits especially costly for the parish. Still, generous health and dental insurance coverage ought to be part of every parish's employment compensation package. Some dioceses require health insurance for employees who work more than a particular number of hours per week, for instance, twenty-five hours; individual states may also legally require it for a certain number of work hours per week. Whatever may be required by diocese or statute, *generous* coverage means that the person employed feels secure in the event of either a passing condition or a lingering illness, perhaps with a small co-pay. Family coverage also ought to be cheap for those who need it. Even the grade school principal, if he has five elementary school age children, cannot afford health insurance on a Catholic parish salary. As the

The Purpose of Performance Analysis

» To develop staff competencies
» To do so in the particular ministry context
» To bolster team relationships
» To strengthen ministry and performance planning

deeper pocket, in justice the parish needs to foot the bill. Furthermore, structuring jobs to be part-time so the parish need not pay benefits is baldly unjust in our national economy.

Ministry Planning and Review

Pastors and pastoral associates supervise parish employees so they perform effectively in the workplace. What constitutes hospitable employee supervision, therefore, needs to be a high priority for those on staff exercising a supervisory role.

Performance *appraisal*, a commonplace form of supervision in business and in many parishes, is an "over/under" relationship in which one assumes power over and judges another. Research indicates that it typically effects no change in employee performance, and can even make things worse.

Performance *analysis*, on the other hand, is a form of employee supervision that helps a person become more effective in producing results. As a method, it is based on the as-

The Collegial Quarterly Performance Analysis Session

» reviews staff job responsibilities and intended results
» considers the proportion of the time expenditure
» examines staff member achievements
» reflects on blockages to ministry effectiveness
» discusses possibilities for improvement
» negotiates a plan for the next quarter
» strives for ministry collaboration and supervisor support

sumption that the whole system that is the parish contributes to or hinders effective ministry performance. Carried out in an ongoing, collaborative planning process, this diagnostic approach to job performance in ministry clarifies job expectations, offers perspective on performance weaknesses, elicits the reasons for weaknesses, and deepens the relationship between the supervisor and the staff member.

The purpose of a performance analysis process is to develop competencies in a member of a parish's staff, to do so in context, and thereby to strengthen team relationships and performance planning. Because it assumes that everyone on a parish staff, working in collaboration, contributes to effective or ineffective ministry functioning, performance analysis builds up parish staff members for ministry and mission, aligning performance objectives with results. This process has specific steps.

First, the parish staff member plans his or her work activities, developing an outline of job responsibilities with a time allotment for each. In this outline, job responsibilities are to be gathered under "key result areas," which serve as the organizing principles for the ministry. Employee and supervisor then negotiate a plan of action. The plan is then carried out and a simple time-use record is kept. At the end of each quarter, work responsibilities and the time investment are reviewed by the employee and the supervisor together. Achievements and areas that need improvement are listed. Blocking forces are noted. Improvement possibilities are proposed and negotiated in the quarterly meeting. The key to this system is the quarterly analysis session in which supervisor and staff member review the ministry of the last three months and plan it for the next three months.

This approach, however formally or informally done, keeps everyone well informed about what's happening in the ministry area and with the minister, clarifies job responsibilities, maintains mutual accountability, opens mutual coaching possibilities, and keeps everyone regularly considering the shape of parish ministry as well as the minister's "fit" in the context. It also helps develop a teamwork approach to ministry built on shared insights and skills.

However structured or unstructured performance analysis might be in a parish, hospitably done it will honor the dignity of everyone involved and express communion in the common mission of the parish. In a better way than performance appraisal, performance analysis mirrors the Trinity's hospitality even in employment relationships. Still, insurmountable walls can build even on a parish staff.

THE LIMITS OF JOB SECURITY

As a hospitable employer, the parish strives to offer staff members the freedom to use their talents, shape their ministry, and do their jobs well; the security of deliberate planning, honest and respectful feedback, and the setting of clear limits; and the meeting of ministry staff members' needs by supplying the orientation, training, and resources to accomplish the tasks set out for them. However faithful we may be to these commitments in hospitable justice, there are exceptions even in the parish to assured, indefinite employment. They are a reduction in force (an extreme measure taken for financial reasons), progressive discipline in the workplace, and just cause discharge. While the supervisor and employee, in accord with the commonly recognized rights and responsibilities of each, may have worked out parameters and expectations for the job, and may know thoroughly diocesan and parish employment policy, nonetheless the parish sometimes faces employment relationship breakdown.

The Three Exceptions to Indefinite Employment

» A reduction in force (RIF) for financial reasons
» Progressive discipline leading to dismissal
» Just cause discharge

Reduction in Force

A reduction in force (RIF) is an extreme measure. It requires the organization to give the employees formal written notification of the organization's financial problems and a list of criteria for employee retention. The corporation must then apply the criteria based on objective data, inform the employee about the termination of the employment relationship, and provide the employee an explanation of the criteria's application in the employee's situation. A listing by age of the relevant employee class must be included with the termination letter. Release from employment under these circumstances is usually accompanied by some form of severance.

The RIF is rare, applied only in exceptional circumstances. The process outlined above must be used in all its particulars or the parish becomes vulnerable to job reinstatement and/or legal action.

The RIF is an enormously painful experience for everyone in the workplace, and it spills over into the parish community as well. That is why the RIF is a last-ditch stabilizing action for a financially distressed parish. Yet in our time, given dwindling numbers and subsequent financial constraints, the permissibility of a RIF suggests that all parish employees need to remain attentive to the parish's financial state.

Progressive Discipline

Progressive discipline is imposed when the employer is discontented with an employee's performance and insufficient rectifying change is taking place. It includes at a minimum: an oral warning substantiated by documentation, a written warning outlining necessary changes, a disciplinary action (like suspension without pay), a final written warning that articulates precise criteria for performance improvement, and a time frame for that improvement. It can lead eventually to dismissal, which typically requires the permission of an attorney, the diocesan personnel officer, and the mutual concurrence of both in the decision.

Progressive discipline, painful as it can be, need not move to termination. With a staff member at St. Matthew's, for instance, the bookkeeper went through the progressive discipline process all the way to the final written warning when she demonstrated to Fr. Pete that the system was broken. She then detailed why what Fr. Pete asked was impossible. She not only kept her job, but the whole bookkeeping system improved markedly because the parish took action on the information she provided.

Progressive discipline can be a wake-up call for employee or employer. The process can clarify expectations, change the operation for the better, and preserve a good employee, even if, very often, it leads to the end of the employment relationship.

Discharge for Just Cause

Discharge for just cause—without progressive discipline— can occur in cases of illegal bias or harassment, theft, records falsification, endangering misconduct, insubordination, breach of professional ethics, use of controlled substances in the workplace, public conduct contradicting Church teaching and morals, or gross violations of the employer/employee relationship.

Discharge for just cause also typically requires the concurrence of the pastor, an attorney, and the diocesan personnel officer. If the employee is released, he or she usually retains the option to appeal the decision to mediation and, ultimately, binding arbitration. Every diocese also has a resolution of work-related issues policy that begins with the immediate supervisor and can run all the way up the Chancery chain of command to the diocesan conciliation process.

Parish pastoral leaders and every member of the parish's ministry staff need to understand clearly what misconduct in the workplace is. Fr. Severin, for instance, has a dog. One evening he came to his mailbox to find there a baggie with dog feces in it. A pastoral associate had found the feces near the building entry and in the church, collected it and placed it, with a note, in the pastor's mailbox. He assumed that the feces were from Fr. Severin's dog, and chose this way of letting him know about it. Fr. Severin was amazed that a colleague would do such a thing, especially one who was already in the process of progressive discipline, but he was unsure how to respond. When he mentioned the incident to an attorney six weeks later while in the throes of the pastoral associate's last days of employment, she instantly asked, "Why didn't you fire the person on the spot?"

"I didn't know I could!"

Fr. Severin ought to have known. The pastoral associate, too, ought to have known that placing a plastic bag of feces in the pastor's mailbox is a gross violation of the employer-employee relationship that could place his job in jeopardy.

THE EMPLOYMENT BIBLE

The parish's *Employment Policies Handbook* is the employment bible for the pastor and the pastoral associates. It is the employment bible for the diocesan personnel office as well as for the attorneys who work with pastors and parishes. The pastor, or the pastoral associates in consultation with the pastor, can only exercise employment authority within the confines of published diocesan and parish policies. The pastor typically must either adhere to the handbook policies, or lose the parish's right to insurance, or risk suit. This cold reality gives the pastor huge incentive to follow the policy.

Moreover, the *Employment Policies Handbook* serves as the employment bible for every parish staff member, and is customarily placed in every parish employee's hands. I have seen staff members suffer terrible losses because of their ignorance of fundamental points made in employment handbooks. Repeated refusal to honor a supervisor's specific requests, for instance, or taking candy from school snack supplies when you have been asked not to do so—no one can stubbornly do these things and keep their job. One employee in a reduction in force, for instance, assumed the parish broke a contract. She never signed a severance agreement and took legal action. The arbitrator found against the employee because the employee handbook provided for a reduction in force. The employee lost thousands of dollars because the employee handbook sat unread in a pile somewhere.

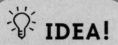

IDEA!

Review the parish employment policy handbook with the councils if it is published.

If the parish *Employment Policies Handbook* is not published or needs revision...

- Invite the councils to approve all parish employment policies, established and revised
- Include in the handbook itself
  - » at each policy section
  - » at each subsequently revised policy
    - + the date of administrative council approval
    - + and the date of pastoral council approval

The enormous importance of the *Employment Policies Handbook* suggests that its composition and contents must not be considered an administrative matter left to the pastor alone. Since the handbook articulates the specific limits to what the pastor and employment supervisor can and cannot do in the employment relationship, draws helpful boundaries for the supervisor/employee relationship for all staff members, and offers guidelines for a parish employee's exercise of power on many levels, both the administrative council and the pastoral council ought to be involved in the handbook approval process. Parishioner pastoral leadership participation in handbook assembly offers the parish significant expertise in the composition process and offers greater assurance that the parish's policies are just and hospitably balanced for all parish employees.

» Accepting American Cultural Reality

The ordinary American presuppositions that parishioners bring to leadership and the simple reality that the parish is an American corporation both offer pastoral leaders and the parish wonderful opportunities. They call pastoral leaders to reflect upon gospel values and church tradition, discuss them, and then come to common agreement about leadership priorities. This reflection and discussion invites everyone to grow in the personal virtue of justice, divine hospitality's ground, asking themselves and one another: what is the right order of relationship that will build up the common good of the parish toward the kingdom? Grappling with American cultural conflicts, therefore, is integral to pastoral leadership. Indeed, the grappling is a great gift that calls everyone to a deeper understanding of their American and ecclesial roots, as well as to a more reflective personal reconciliation of these roots deep within.

— PROCESS QUESTIONS —

1. What is your experience of the differences between American leadership and decision-making presuppositions in relationship to church ones?

2. How do your parish's councils elect their members? What process would you like to see?

3. What do you think of the idea that, as an employer, your parish is subject essentially to the same rules and guidelines as IBM or General Motors?

4. What thought have you ever given before to the fact that your pastor's responsibilities are just like that of a small or medium size business owner's?

CHAPTER 10

A School: Creative Tension for a Parish

» Education Culture and Parish Culture

A parochial school graces and strains a parish community like no other ministry. I was pastor of two parishes with schools. One parish supported the school ministry vigorously, the other, a merger of two parishes with shrinking schools, was ambivalent about it. In both parishes, many families with children in the school, and some parishioners outside that community, touted the school as the parish's central mission. While educating and forming children is at least as much a gift as it is a responsibility for a parish, the tendency to supersize the school ministry's importance, fog its purpose, isolate it from the rest of the parish, compete for parish resources, and seek domination over other ministries creates stress for all parishes with schools. Balanced perspective on the school ministry's proper place in the parish's ministry life challenges every parish community with a school.

Many areas of conflict compound ordinary relationship difficulties in a parish with a school. Three will be addressed here: the tendency to see the school as a separate institution instead of a parish ministry, the proper relationship balance between the principal and the pastor, and the governance structure that best serves the parish and the school.

NOT A SEPARATE INSTITUTION, BUT A PARISH MINISTRY

Most parishioners and pastoral leaders, as well as parents with children in the parish school, markedly tend to treat a school as an entity separate from the parish. This sense of separation begins with language. Common parish language refers to "the school" and "the parish" or "the church." The plant speaks of separateness; the school is typically in its own building, and sometimes across the street or down the block from the church and offices. A sense of separation is further emphasized by the typical school faculty. The teaching staff tends to be understandably clubby and is inclined to hold itself apart from the rest of the parish staff. The teaching staff tends as well to give its loyalty to the principal over and against the pastor. It is also common that, even if they are Catholic, most teachers belong to parishes other than the one in which they teach; many of them feel ambivalent about their faith, too, certainly much more so than the women religious teachers of the past.

The sheer visibility of a school ministry compared to other parish's ministries—nearly 200 days of children, parents, patrols, visiting teams, traffic—also contributes vividly to the sense of the school's being both prominent in itself and separate from the parish. The focused intensity parents have for their children, the great commonality children and parents share in a school setting, the singularity of a school calendar, the regimentation of the school day—all these factors contribute to the pervasive sense that the school is "other than" in the vast majority of parishes. Because many families with children in the parish school disconnect their school commitment from their parish commitment—participating faithfully in school activities but haphazardly in Sunday Eucharist and Sunday stewardship—the sense of separation between "the school" and "the church" can feel almost complete. Most pastoral leaders across the country acquiesce to this sense of separation because it can seem so natural. Accepting this sense of separation, however, is a contrary sign within the parish and to the world.

Governed by the parish's articles of incorporation, a school is one ministry among all those of the parish. Indeed, the fundamental justification for a parish having a school is formation in faith, not education. That was the parochial school's original purpose beginning in the 1850s. As immigrants arrived on our shores, parish schools multiplied across the nation and were mandated in the 1880s, so that the church might educate them to thrive in American culture, yes, but primarily to form the generations for participation in the life of the American Catholic Church. That remains our justifying purpose today: forming children in worship, the Catholic tradition, spirituality, gracious attentiveness to other people's needs, living and valuing community, charitable work, and social justice principles and action. These gifts are the parish's specifically gospel-based ministry to its schoolchildren. As a community of faith, the parish owes the children this ministry far more than it owes them instruction in math, science, and social studies. The parish's school ministry will do that instruction well because of our tradition's staunch and venerable commitment to educational excellence and the liberal arts. Still, the school's primary mission is gospel ministry formation, followed up immediately, as left hand to right, by a fine liberal arts education.

To approach the point with blunt clarity: the parish school is a derivative ministry. It is a justifiable ministry for the parish insofar as it forms children and families in worship, religious education, spirituality, justice, charity, and the values of community life. Insofar as a school ministry misses the mark on this formation, then just so far is the parish's investment in it unjustified, no matter how fine the education. Pastoral leaders, consequently, need to shift language usage, staff relationships, and governance structures so they clearly demonstrate that the school is a ministry of the parish.

A CASE IN POINT

Fr. Frank became pastor of Nativity of John the Baptist, a parish chest-busting proud of its elementary education tradition. He saw immediately, however, the school's strident sense of separation from the parish. Not only did he hear this in ordinary discourse, but he also read in the school's public relations materials that the school was private and Christian, not parochial and Catholic. The principal indicated clearly that she expected little to no connection with Fr. Frank. The school board set the school's tuition, staff salaries, and budget, and the competition for the parish's financial resources was fierce. The school board meetings consistently descended into parents putting the principal on the spot about day-to-day school matters, including curriculum and discipline.

Convinced that the school was a parish ministry, Fr. Frank began to talk about that. Carefully, slowly he won over the principal, largely because Fr. Frank stood against her being put on the spot in school board meetings. When the middle school religion teacher retired, the pastoral associate for religious formation consented to revise and teach a core religion curriculum in the middle school, with an eye toward eventually winning over the faculty enough to reshape the elementary and intermediate religion curriculum as well. The pastoral associate for worship consented to complement the new middle school curriculum with a liturgical music and history session each week. Fr. Frank gradually took all bookkeeping, technology assistance, and public relations services for all of the parish's ministries into the parish's main office. He also modified the school board's place in the budget process by asserting that, while the board could offer input, it was the proper role of the administrative and pastoral councils to approve the parish ministry budget, and that included the school.

All the while, as the pastor, principal, pastoral staff, and other pastoral leaders reflected and conferred together about facts on the ground, they decided to shift language to clarify even further that the school was a parish ministry. They began to call the school "the school ministry." They modified the street signs that said "Nativity of John the Baptist School" and "Nativity of John the Baptist Church" to say simply "Nativity of John the Baptist." Since it provided facilities for religious education as well as the school ministry program, they began referring to "the classroom building" instead of "the school." After they succeeded in moving the parish offices into the building, they began to refer to it as "the ministry center," and had that name placed above a new main entry. Eventually, the school board voted itself out of existence and, on the way out, voted a school ministry commission in to replace it.

All of these changes, done over eight years, got people's attention. Staff and parishioners talked and asked about them. Occasionally there were irritable exchanges, and some expressed fears that the school was losing its importance. Still, two pastors later, the changes remain and Nativity of John the Baptist continues to grow more and more deeply into a clear sense that the school is a ministry of the parish, not a separate institution.

The parish school's first mission as a ministry of the parish is to form children and families in the worship, teaching, ideas, relationship patterns, customs, history, and even physical effects of the Christian community, the Catholic Church, and Catholic culture. Pastoral staff members assuming responsibility for areas of the school ministry's life—one shaping the religion curriculum and teaching in it, another offering liturgy and music instruction and preparing the children for worship, another supervising community service to parish elderly who need help with yard work, and so on—tells the children, their parents, and parishioners at large that the school is a ministry of the parish. Keeping basic school ministry planning and budget approval in the hands of the councils does the same. Surrounding the children with quality religious art, an atmosphere of visual quiet and personal calm, hiring faculty and administrators committed to the faith, visits from pastoral leaders, an across-curriculum commitment to community service, non-shaming, respectful and attentively formational discipline that honors every child's dignity—all these things integrate a school within the parish's gospel ministries. Parishes with schools need to proclaim in word and act, and on every level of their life, that the school is not a separate institution, but a ministry of the parish.

The Hallmarks of a Parish School Ministry's Catholic Identity

Regular Eucharist and other liturgical worship

A Catholic administrator

A large majority of practicing Catholics on the faculty

Pastoral associates engaged in teaching:
- religious studies,
- liturgy and liturgical music
- community service

Council oversight of governance policies and finances

Parent participation in governance and policy-making

Non-shaming and respectfully formational discipline

Differentiated instruction

A carefully structured and focused religion curriculum

Sacramental preparation integrated with the whole parish

Commitment to community service

Religious art throughout the environment

A spirit of quiet and order in the building

Building use for parish ministries other than the school

THE PRINCIPAL: PASTORAL ASSOCIATE, NOT LONE WOLF

The relationship between the pastor and principal has an enormous impact on the integration of the school into the gospel ministry life of the parish, and vice versa. Consequently, the relationship between the pastor and the principal requires particular and careful consideration.

The Accurate Title

The title *principal*, with its strong disciplinary undertone in the culture of education, suggests that the position's occupant enjoys a kind of independence that he or she simply does not have in a parish school ministry. Carrying out the logic of the education culture title *principal* within a parochial school setting would demand this understanding: if the head of the school ministry is the principal, with the full intensity of that title's meaning, then the pastor is the parish school's superintendent. This language clarifies the roles, but is practically unworkable in a parish context.

The principal in a parish setting, therefore, might most accurately be titled *pastoral associate for education/principal*, nomenclature that acknowledges the position's proper place in both parish and education culture. By indicating clearly the principal's immediate relationship with the pastor, intimate connection with the pastoring ministry, and collegial relationship with the other pastoral associates, the title *pastoral associate for education/principal* accurately mirrors its holder's relational context and priorities. This clarity is as helpful for the principal as it is for parents with children in the school, pastoral leadership, and the parishioners at large.

Roles and Collegial Relationship

The pastoral associate for education/principal, however, holds a unique position among the parish's pastoral leaders. Unlike other pastoral associates, a principal supervises from eleven to forty people or more, manages a seven-digit budget, supervises the arrangement and maintenance of 30,000 square feet of space, serves a large and passionately interested constituency, and is entrusted with the security and future of the parish's children for seven hours a day, nearly 200 days a year. The principal, therefore, has considerable authority and power, and builds on that through his or her educational leadership. Moreover, if the pastor is the generalist on the ministry staff for the parish as a whole, the principal is the generalist on the school ministry staff for the school ministry as a whole.

Like the other pastoral associates—liturgy and music, religious education, pastoral care—the principal also has an esoteric mystique. The principal is a specialist: the educator's educator, the disciplinarian's disciplinarian, and the employment supervisor of a large staff. The size of the principal's responsibility and the context of the office's exercise, consequently, demand that the pastor and principal collaborate in a particularly sensitive way. The wise and collegial pastor will acknowledge, respect, and honor the principal's singular leadership role and hard-won expertise. Not doing so disrespects the principal's mandate.

At the same time, the pastor oversees the gospel mission and vision of the whole parish, including the school ministry. Furthermore, the pastor remains inalienably accountable for all matters of law, property, personnel, and finances in the parish. The pastor also supervises the pastoral associate for education/principal as employer. Consequently, the wise pastoral associate for education/principal works in a closely cooperative relationship with the pastor day to day, takes the pastor's cues seriously, strives for common vision, and accepts coaching on the pastor's inalienable responsibilities. Not to do so can wreak havoc in a parish and pulls the rug out from under the pastor and pastoral associate's relationship.

A CASE IN POINT

Fr. Martin went on sabbatical. Before he left he worked closely with the pastoral associate for education/principal and both councils to establish the school ministry budget for the next year—tuition, salary raises, program expenses—within the whole parish budget. Three months into the sabbatical, the parish's interim administrator called Fr. Martin to tell him that faculty members had stirred up parents to increase faculty salaries and parents were meeting in one another's homes to garner support. The principal, he told the pastor, was meeting with the parent groups and agreed with their point of view. By phone, Fr. Martin laid out with the interim administrator and trustees principles for settling parent concerns that allowed for an unanticipated but just salary increase. He refrained from contacting the pastoral associate for education/principal, however, because his breach of Fr. Martin's trust might have led to an angry exchange that could have thwarted the process. Nor did the pastoral associate for education/principal make any explanatory call to Fr. Martin. When the interim administrator and councils settled their work, Fr. Martin initiated a frank discussion with the pastoral associate. Fr. Martin made it clear that the pastoral associate had violated his responsibility to publicly support a budget he had consensually agreed to with the councils, and he violated his relationship of trust with the pastor and councils not only by doing that, but also by publicly siding with the parents. Tension eased considerably when the pastoral associate for education/principal, finally comprehending the relationship rupture and its meaning, had the good sense to resign voluntarily.

If the pastoral associate for education/principal serves the mission of the parish as articulated by the councils and led by the pastor, and takes the pastor's coaching regarding law, personnel, property, and finances, then he or she will shine in the parish like a new penny. If the pastor respects and honors the pastoral associate for education/principal's expertise, coaches gently and sagaciously, backs up the pastoral associate and trusts him or her, then the pastor serves well the pastoral associate, the school ministry, and the parish. But when the monarch and the duke contend, civil war is the ever-threatening and unhappy result.

SCHOOL MINISTRY GOVERNANCE: COUNCILS AND COMMISSION, NOT SCHOOL BOARD

In the U.S., the public school board is a legal entity whose authority is based on the independent incorporation of the school or schools under its jurisdiction. Its role is to provide general direction and oversight to an educational institution. Unless a Catholic school is independently incorporated—true for most high schools and elementary schools that belong to clustered parishes, but not for the vast majority of parish schools—the use of the term *school board* is a misnomer. The term *school board* sets up its members with misleading expectations and contrary presuppositions, which inevitably bring it into conflict with the pastor and councils. Worse, a board often sets itself against the pastoral associate for education/principal because its members, left unchecked, ask questions-without-boundaries that hold

the pastoral associate publicly accountable for relatively pica-
yune matters, matters usually and rightfully belonging to the
pastoral associate for education/principal's office, or within his
or her relationship with the pastor.

The School Ministry and the Councils

A parish's school ministry is cared for most properly in just the
same way and with the exactly the same leadership structures
as the parish's other ministries. The parish's pastoral council
oversees the school's long-range planning, evaluates it as a ministry of the parish, and both monitors and makes recommendations about its financial, legal, property, and personnel aspirations and developments. The parish's administrative council
sets school ministry tuition, recommends staff raises or freezes
in accord with those recommended for the whole parish staff,
establishes its budget, consults with the pastor and pastoral
associate about the personnel and legal issues that arise, and
monitors the school ministry's building and property maintenance. Both bodies see to it that the school ministry's personnel policies, legal practices, and fundraising policies cohere
consistently with those of the rest of the parish's ministries.
Mindful of the financial proportion of a school ministry in a
parish budget, and the large number of persons affected by it,
a school ministry still most properly receives the same focus,
guidance, and monitoring by the councils as do all of the other
ministries of the parish.

The School Ministry Commission

Included within the parish's care for the school as a ministry, the pastoral associate for education/principal establishes
an advisory commission of parents and friends to help sustain meaningful parent involvement, an effective development program, and policy regularity about a wide variety

of school ministry matters, for example, uniform policy, transportation policy, and children's safety. The school ministry commission belongs to the pastoral associate for education/principal. It assists with the basics of school ministry planning, which would include forging a school ministry mission statement complementary to that of the parish, shaping school ministry goals and objectives complementary to those of the parish, developing budget scenarios that help the administrative council set tuition and recommend salary raises, offering staff expansion or contraction options that support curriculum development, establishing code of conduct policies so they reflect the school's unique personality as well as its gospel ministry standards, and setting school ministry goals regarding enrollment. In the areas of policy and practice, ministry and money, the school min-

The School Board

» legal entity
» established by law
» jurisdictional and regulatory
» belongs to constituents
» directs the institution
» impact directed to locality
» elected by majority or appointed
» committed to school mission
» acts on constituents' behalf

The School Ministry Commission

» participation entity
» established by pastor and pastoral associate
» consultative
» belongs to pastoral associate for education/ principal
» focuses, guides, and monitors the parish's school ministry program
» impact mindful of whole church
» elected by discernment
» committed to school mission
» under the umbrella of the parish's mission
» acts for the good of the whole and only within commission meetings

istry commission assists the pastoral associate for education/ principal to focus, guide, and monitor the school as a parish ministry, and helps to keep the school ministry accountable to parish pastoral leadership.

Parishes have no boards but the corporate board. Parish school ministry governance concerns are most appropriately and effectively handled by the parish's ordinary structures: collegial relationship with the pastor and pastoral staff, the pastoral council, the administrative council, and the school ministry commission.

THE SCHOOL MINISTRY: A FINAL WORD

Consensus about the purpose of the parish school has broken down in our time. Catholic elementary education will likely not rebound until a new consensus is achieved. That will take time. Those of us in Catholic education strive to articulate a clear purpose, but the purpose we have articulated thus far remains less than compelling in an age when the church hangs out on the sidelines of family life.

Yet, parish school ministry remains a marvelous opportunity. If the religion curriculum is deeply rooted in the heart of the tradition and focused on the ground of our faith—the Scriptures, Jesus, Creed, Sacraments, the Sacred Liturgy, and the vast sweep of church history—then even the students have the potential to inspire parents to regular participation in Eucharist and growing in faith by merely asking their parents for help with their religion homework. Involvement in the parish school secures for many parents and children a deep, lifetime commitment to the high value of community life. Indeed, one of the crucial functions of a parochial school is long-term rather than immediate. Memories of school ministry hospitality— worship, religious education, spiritual formation, pastoral care, community life, and Catholic culture—surface later to invite people who have shared in school ministry life to come back again to the table of the Lord even after years of being away from church.

In sum, the enormous richness of possibility for a parish's school ministry warrants clear articulation of the school's mission as a ministry of the parish, mutually respectful structuring of the relationship between the pastoral associate for education/principal and the pastor, and vigilant attention to the school's integration in every way into the parish's pastoral leadership life. Hospitality to our children and our families with children in the school ministry calls us to this noble work not only for the short run, but in hope accomplishing God's work in the long haul as well.

— PROCESS QUESTIONS —

1. Is your school one of the parish's ministries or separate from it?

2. What is the parish's budget process relative to school ministry's tuition, salaries, and program expenses?

3. What level of participation do families with children in the school ministry have in the parish's life?

4. What connection does the parish staff have with what happens in the school ministry?

Bringing Hands Together in Prayer and Work

» One Hand Not Knowing What the Other is Doing

As we ponder our hands left and right, and as we experience and reflect upon collaboration and collegiality among lay and ordained in ministry relationship, the call to gospel mission demands that we ask ourselves: how do we bring our hands together in prayer and work so that we might transform our lives and the world according to the pattern of life Jesus has shown us? As I stated at the beginning of this book, the place to go to examine possible responses to this question is, simply, reality.

ONE HAND: THE LAITY

Research studies by James Davidson, Dean Hoge and others (*American Catholics Today*, Rowman & Littlefield, 2007) tell us that seventy-one percent of laypeople in the U.S. believe they should have a role in selecting their pastors. Eighty-nine percent of the laity in our parishes expect to be involved in

decisions about their parish's finances. Clearly the vast majority of Catholic laypeople accept the Vatican II-inspired view
that the laity, in virtue of the baptism that lay and ordained
share, should have an active rather than a passive role in their
church.

Laypeople link this view of their role to a servant-leader understanding of the priest's role, a conceptualization in which
priest and parishioner, equal before God in their baptism yet
functioning within their respective roles, collaborate together
to shape the church's life, for example, in liturgy planning, religious education, and finances.

Servant Leadership

A new moral principle is emerging which
holds that the only authority deserving
one's allegiance is that which is freely
and knowingly granted by the led to the
leader in response to, and in proportion to,
the clearly evident servant stature of the
leader...[people] will freely respond only to
individuals who are chosen as leaders because
they are proven and trusted as servants.

» ROBERT K. GREENLEAF,
SERVANT LEADERSHIP, P. 10

ONE HAND: THE ORDAINED

Research on priests (*Evolving Visions of the Priesthood*, The
Liturgical Press, 2003) shows that while those ordained in the

1960s and 1970s hold similar convictions to those of the laity, the attitudes of priests ordained in the 1980s and since diverge. The so-called "John Paul II priests" and "Benedict XVI priests" understand their ministry in what is called *cultic* rather than servant-leadership terms. They see Holy Orders, not baptism, as the role-defining sacrament in the church. In the cultic view of priesthood, Holy Orders sets the ordained apart to serve the church by celebrating the sacraments, teaching the truths of the faith, and governing the church's life. Precisely this point of view underlies the post-ordination hand-kissing story in chapter 2. The cultic view of priesthood implicitly assumes that the laity's role is subordinate to that of the ordained, and the ordained therefore exercise ultimate authority in the church's life, even in administrative decision making.

One can quickly surmise that this striking divergence leaves the American laity and the American ordained out of sync. The church needs both hands in coordination, however, in order to be church effectively. Indeed, both hands of the church's gospel ministry in the U.S. can be brought into happy and effective coordination.

» A Both/And, Both Hand Model
ACCEPTING REALITY

The Christian spiritual tradition across the centuries calls out to us: "Know thyself." Self knowledge before God grounds the spiritual life and spiritual growth. If we know ourselves as we are, then we can, in humility, accept God's acceptance of us as we are, commend ourselves as we are into God's hands, come to know what we need to ask from God and sort through to where in our lives we need to apply the discipline necessary to grow. "Grace builds on nature," Thomas Aquinas says. Reality, what is, "simple fact," is the first building block for our growth into the pattern of life Jesus has shown us.

Yet, we humans sometimes, perhaps often, work to avoid reality. We hold that something is the opposite of what it is, we decide it simply does not exist, we project our weaknesses onto others; we act out, we hide, we do something else; we deny reality, we blame others and we numb ourselves with food, drink, chemicals, sex, shopping, or gambling. When we try to escape reality, what is, "simple fact," we risk losing ourselves and God, who created reality. Reality avoidance always inhibits human growth.

Facing what is, as it is, frees us humans because reality is the solid and sole foundation upon which we can build our future in God by giving ourselves over to God as we are. In our spiritual tradition, accepting reality, what is, "simple fact"—the essence of what our tradition means by humility—is always the starting point for growth in the divine hospitality.

PASTOR REALITY

Seminary education trains priests to preside at liturgy; to be theologically accurate and attentive, and perhaps even astute and articulate; and to offer competent pastoral care. Everyone who functions in the pastor role, even if not ordained, has been trained in the last two areas at least. The ordained receive no organizational management training in seminary, however, unless by chance they have it from elsewhere or are experienced pastors, though these, too, have usually learned their skills through experience alone.

Pastor reality in parish life across the church is reasonably clear. Every parish in the world is assigned to a priest pastor, even if an occasional deacon or layperson administers it with a pastor's attendant rights and responsibilities. According to canon and corporate law, the pastor (or administrator if delegated) holds full responsibility for the whole organization. The pastor holds inalienable accountability for all matters of personnel, law, finances, and property, as well as for the faith and morals of the parish community. Ordained and/or appointed into an extended hierarchical system, the pastor is a family member in the family business. Real power belongs to the pastor by right, and the pastor distributes it by extending the divine hospitality for the sake spreading God's goodness to the ends of the earth—gospel ministry.

One must also note: the church expects that the pastor, as one of his major responsibilities, assists the lay faithful to exercise their proper role in the gospel mission.

THE LAITY'S REALITY

Lay reality is also reasonably clear. Parishioners are well-educated, highly skilled, affluent, and confident. They have long experience with managing money, running businesses, marketing products, selling services, consulting about organizational change, knowing the law, hiring and firing people, managing staff, teaching children and adults, implementing education programs, and shaping superb communications. In their daily lives, the laity lead and they understand organization—from gathering the extended family for dinner to working with the corporate board to compose the corporation's mission statement. Our laypeople are well-educated to exercise these responsibilities.

Our laity can also be expected to understand perceptively their own reality. Whether that reality be the day-to-day stresses of transporting children thither and yon, or the significant cultural differences Latinos experience among Colombians, Ecuadorians, Peruvians, Mexicans, and Bolivians, our laypeople have broad sensibilities and deep sensitivities to their own life experience that offer utterly reliable perspective for shaping effective pastoral leadership.

Many of our laypeople also feel shy about functioning in liturgy and teaching the content of faith. Still, they want to be involved, are most often a quick study, and enjoy being equipped for ministry.

BRINGING TWO HANDS TOGETHER

Reasonable people would conclude from reality that the gifts and lacks of the laity and the ordained complement each other in such a way that each needs what the other has and has what the other needs for whole, effective pastoral leadership. Bringing lay and ordained together so that one hand folds beautifully into the other hand as if in prayer, so that one hand supports the other effectively in common work, requires some letting go on the part of both the ordained and the laity.

The Pastor's Call

Effective pastoral leadership calls the pastor to seek out God's abounding gifts among the people, appreciate them as gifts, and strive to use them to build a parish vision, the parish's particular way of implementing gospel ministry. If the pastor trusts the gifts of the people, structures the organization to use these gifts for big-picture purposes (planning, discernment and focusing, guiding and monitoring the parish's gospel ministry life), shares with the gifted clearly delineated and real responsibility, confides in them, and joins together with the group for the gift distribution, then the pastor exercises genuinely hospitable pastoral leadership. If the pastor withholds, then the mutuality of the guest/host relationship—the divine hospitality—is undone; God's gifts are refused.

The Staff's and Parishioners' Call

Effective pastoral leadership calls those surrounding the pastor to see the pastor's gifts, to appreciate them as they are, and strive to complement them in such a way that they support the pastor in shaping them to build a parish vision, the parish's particular way of implementing gospel ministry. If those around the pastor trust the pastor's gifts, help to structure the organization so the pastor's gifts can be used for big-picture purposes (joining in planning toward a parish vision, discerning parish direction in collegial relationship, and overseeing the focusing, guiding, and monitoring gospel ministry life), accept real responsibility and its limits, keep the pastor's confidence, and join together with the pastor in the gift distribution, then those surrounding the pastor exercise genuinely hospitable pastoral leadership. If those surrounding the pastor withhold, then the divine hospitality is undone; God's gifts are refused.

Imagine for a moment one hand clapping. The church in the United States needs both hands clapping. Otherwise, gospel ministry fails. But what does this coming together of both hands in prayer and work look like?

» Pastoral Leadership's Three Points of Approach

Pastoral leadership plans, gives itself over to God's purposes through consensus decision making, extends divine hospitality, and does so trustingly around the third table of parish life in such a manner that people's lives and the world are transformed according to the pattern of life Jesus has shown us. That is gospel ministry. Different positions in the community of faith, however, offer different possibilities and limits for approaching effective pastoral leadership. So, how might a pastoral council member, a pastoral associate, or the pastor approach it?

A PARISHIONER PASTORAL COUNCIL MEMBER'S APPROACH

Urging Pastoral Planning

A pastoral council member's first approach would be to help the council see the need to engage in pastoral planning. The planning process itself, over time, offers the forum for building trust in the parish and addressing the parish's main concerns and their subtexts. Engagement in a parish's real issues—safely, gently, carefully structured over time within the planning process—brings direction and vision to any parish. Pastoral planning offers great hope to a parish in any situation, and a parishioner council member is in an excellent position to urge it.

Structuring Planning

If pastoral planning is not central and ongoing in the life of the parish pastoral council, then council members need to advocate for it. If a pastoral council consents to planning, then its selection of a process (see Appendix 2 on page 244) automatically confronts it with questions about its size and composition. The council then has three alternatives: either plan with the group as it is, reshape the group, or plan with a committee of the council. Planning with a larger group, even a cumbersome one, has the distinct advantage of building broader consensus among more people. Consensus building is the aim of the process, after all. Reshaping the council into an "elected" membership of about nine people may delay planning, but will be well worth it. Committee-delegated planning has the advantage of greater efficiency and a more quickly produced product. It requires, however, double-discussion of many issues because council members get stuck on particular concerns that planning documents raise, and they need to process committee proposals at some length. Still, various group arrangements can serve pastoral planning's purpose of building a parish vision admirably by beginning the work of coming to consensus around a parish's identity, image, mission, and direction.

Planning also requires a schedule, at a minimum, of two meetings a month ten months a year. That's eighteen meetings per year. The council would need to be urged to adopt this schedule because anything less stops planning momentum and dooms the process.

Mindful of Muhammad's three gates, and attentive to avoiding obnoxiousness, pastoral planning and its required schedule need to be urged until the council sees it as its main purpose.

What About the Pastor?

If a council member wins the pastor over to planning, shifting the council's mission becomes relatively easy. Still, if the council were to approve it, most pastors would be content to let planning happen. Fully comprehending its purpose and value might be beyond the pastor, but outright objection is unlikely. While getting a pastor's consent may require on-the-side attempts to persuade people around the pastor as well as the pastor, building a head of steam in this way for council planning's sake is worth the effort to accomplish the end result.

If Fr. Archie from Sts. Peter and Paul, met in chapter 4, were pastor—a pious and kindly man, but lacking in self-confidence, and consequently defensive and fearful of losing control—assuring conversations on the side would likely help calm him. Conviction in the chair and others that the process is valuable, and consistent assurances and perspective throughout the process that points to its value, would likely bring Fr. Archie to ease in the long run.

The response from Fr. Biff, pastor of St. Damasus, also met in chapter 4, would be dicey. Control is his issue, and he has a marked tendency to make snap decisions because he prefers to be busy about things other than the parish. Pastoral planning, done in a spiritually grounded, discerning way, puts the Holy Spirit in control and requires, at a minimum, the pastor's approval. If Fr. Biff publicly demurred from planning, a private approach to him through one or more of his inner circle, if they are themselves persuadable, would likely persuade him. If he shuts down altogether, a council power play that reaches for planning would likely backfire.

...be wily as serpents and gentle as doves.

» MATTHEW 10:16B

If pastoral planning fails to fly, if it needs to be set aside for awhile, do that. Its day will come and persistence will win out, though it may take years for an idea to take hold enough to be seriously considered. The wait is worth it because the council's choosing to set planning as its first priority would change parish life, and the pastor's approval, even if less than hearty participation, would energize the process. Good discussions, insightful focus groups, accurate data, and practically workable goals and objectives would likely, in themselves, inspire the council in its work and entice the pastor into the process more and more deeply over time. People always want to associate themselves with apparent success. Patience will win the day.

Urging Discernment Decision Making

A second and closely associated approach for a pastoral leadership group member would be to urge the pastoral or administrative council to adopt spiritually grounded consensus decision making. A commitment to consensus decision making in council can serve as a first, basic step toward the process of consensus-building among all the parishioners around parish vision and direction. Commitment to seeking what God wants of us and what we can live with deepens council experience around even mundane matters, and opens it to the Holy Spirit's power. The more fully the council commits itself to consensus decision making, the more completely it opens itself to God's work for and within the parish.

Other Modest Options?

Moving the pastoral leadership group meetings to a low table and bringing in snacks so as to warm relationships can be helpful steps toward reaching for pastoral planning and discernment decision making in any pastoral leadership group. Commission level pastoral planning and discernment decision making help as well, requiring tactics similar to those council members might use in working with the pastor.

Meeting observers outside pastoral leadership groups may be able to have some impact. Non-membership in a pastoral leadership group, however, diminishes to a trickle the possibilities for a non-member to contribute to a group's or the parish's transformation. Pecking at a council or a commission in open meetings to achieve these ends alienates more than it wins cooperation. Subterfuge and agitation hurt people.

Within a pastoral leadership group, however, implementing a substantial pastoral planning process and discernment decision making provide all the leaven the pastoral council needs to bring about, in time, parish grounding, centering, and focus. The planning and decision-making processes might well be bumpy. Nonetheless, winning the implementation of these steps in the group's process will very likely turn the ignition key to God's work in pastoral leadership and the parish.

Do it. Trust it. Then let God be God for the rest. But remember: these humble steps reach the limits of what a parishioner pastoral leadership group member can accomplish, unless he or she has remarkable powers of persuasion with persons elsewhere in parish leadership.

A PASTORAL ASSOCIATE'S PASTORAL LEADERSHIP APPROACH

A pastoral staff member's effective pastoral leadership approach within a parish rests in three areas: clarity about the ministry description, the pastoral staff meeting, and the ministry commission's planning and process.

Honoring the Ministry Description

Competence, professionalism, transparent accountability, sound relationships (including cautious personal boundaries and attentiveness to self need), and the singular desire to do what God wants in the ministry area—these dispositions make pastoral staff members indispensable colleagues in ministry. With these gifts solidly in place, any pastor, any parish would be delighted with a pastoral associate's performance.

Building trust with the pastor requires all of the above, plus conversations with the pastor about the pastor's vision of the ministry area, consistent offers to share ministry information and plans with the pastor in advance, and respect for the pastor's confidence about pastor response to practical, day-to-day staff and parishioner "awkwardnesses"...and they abound. With these practices in place, most pastors become affable colleagues.

Pastoral associates also need to keep close and clear communication with the pastor regarding any questions about their position's limits, and sometimes about other staff members' position limits as well. Pastoral staff members need to remain vigilant about colleague temptations to overstep limits or to invite others to do the same. Clarity about one's own ministry description, and others', helps keep parish staff members happy and effective.

Taking Advantage of the Pastoral Staff Meeting

Pastoral staff meetings provide the pastoral associate opportunity to address from a pastoral point of view the parish's priority concerns, its direction and vision, and what good order in the office ought to look like. Each of these concerns, tactfully and congenially but consistently questioned and probed, can open the whole staff's minds and hearts to seeing the parish's main concerns, to understanding the value of pastoral planning and discernment decision making, to moving the whole parish toward hospitality as its major commitment, and to understanding the grounding and focus for pastoral leadership on every level. The pastoral associate sits in the proper chair for asking over and over the question, "What is our mission?" Discussing possible answers to this question can, within the staff meeting, over time, shape the entire staff's reflection and action. This gradual transformation can also spill over into the councils and the parish as a whole.

Offering the Ministry Commission as an Example to the Parish

Through the ministry commission, a pastoral associate can demonstrate with aplomb all of the major elements of Good News pastoral leadership: the planning, discernment decision making, hospitality extending, and trust building that shape a parish's vision and direction.

A CASE IN POINT

Mary Catherine, pastoral associate for education/prin-
cipal of Fr. Biff's parish, St. Damasus, met in chapter 4
and above, determined that the school ministry would
engage in pastoral planning. Fr. Biff and the business administrator both thought it was a waste of time. Mary
Catherine went ahead anyway.

To justify the planning process from the start, and
to make a point with it, Mary Catherine gave the school
ministry commission an assignment. She asked them
to imagine they were looking for a school for their
child. She then asked them to consider this question:
What five statements, if you heard them upon visiting a
school, would be so compelling you would immediately
want to enroll your child?

After compiling the results and choosing the top eight
responses, Mary Catherine listed them out as statements
about St. Damasus, and then engaged the group in a gap
analysis using this question: How is St. Damasus different from these statements? The exercise finished with
a marvelous listing of who St. Damasus is and what it
does, and where it needs to grow.

When Mary Catherine showed the exercise results to
them, both Fr. Biff and the business administrator saw
the value of the exercise. The listing also had the happy
effect of putting Fr. Biff's concern about the school ministry's Catholic identity to rest.

The pastoral staff member's approach always needs to be
doing what he or she can do in the best way possible. For while
a pastoral associate cannot control the culture of the parish, the
approach of the pastor, what happens in the councils, or how

the whole staff interacts, he or she can influence the whole parish's gospel ministry quite significantly by the manner in which he or she approaches ministry.

> What you cannot make good, make at least as little bad as you can.
>
> » ST. THOMAS MORE

THE PASTOR'S APPROACH

The pastor has, of course, the greatest freedom to act, and can do so on several fronts simultaneously. The pastoral council can be jumpstarted to begin pastoral planning, implement discernment decision making, set a momentum-sustaining number of meetings and close meetings to parishioner visitors. The pastor can also reshape council membership to render the group's process effective, thereby creating a forum and long-haul structure for reflecting on the parish's major unresolved questions. This activity with the councils eventually builds trust, vision, and direction for the community so long as the pastor remains actively engaged in it.

Following employment policies properly, the pastor may also reshape the parish's staff, or reshape staff ministry descriptions, so staff members follow clearly delineated responsibilities and duties, and respect limits. The pastor should hold everyone on staff accountable for fulfilling his or her ministry description, and is free to proceed with progressive discipline in the event of failure.

If the parish's worship is alive and open to the Spirit's wind and fire within it, and if its governance is in order with planning, discernment, hospitality, and trust-building focused toward shaping the parish's vision and direction, then the parish community will be well fed from all three tables where heaven and earth meet in parish life.

All of these actions on the pastor's part, coupled with simple presence on site and at parish events, open the whole parish to hospitable, effective gospel ministry.

» Four Ongoing Exercises that Keep Hands in Coordination

In the end, four ongoing exercises in parish life bring all hands together in prayer and work: pastoral planning, discernment decision making, extending hospitality, and building trust.

PASTORAL PLANNING

Vision never simply emerges in a parish, nor can it be mandated. Vision is built. Coming together in an ordered process to plan for the parish's future builds its vision. The process of pastoral planning, therefore, needs always to be in place. It engages the pastor and leadership together in continually learning from the past, reflecting actively on the present and moving out toward the future. An active, optimistic, forward moving, life-giving process, pastoral planning generates hope for the future and trust in present pastoral leadership. The creativity, insight and personal engagement the process demands calls the best out of pastoral leaders and opens them up to

The Four Essential Elements of Good News Pastoral Leadership

- » Ongoing pastoral planning
- » Discernment decision making
- » Broad and gracious hospitality
- » Trust

surprising possibilities. If all parish pastoral leaders engage as equals in pastoral planning, then their every meeting around the third table of parish life can be transforming.

DISCERNMENT DECISION MAKING

When Jesus gives us his prayer, he asks us to commend our whole lives, without reserve or nuance, into the Father's hands: Thy will be done. We are a people about the business, Jesus teaches us, of discerning the gifts and the demands of our relationship with God. Discernment is our way of life as a Christian people. Discernment of the past's meaning, discernment of the present, discernment toward the future, is a way of life for effective pastoral leaders.

When the pastor and pastoral leadership gather to ask together, "What is it that God wants of us?" they model, for the parish and for the world, faithfulness to the first question of the spiritual life. When they struggle with the question, "Can I live with this decision?" they proclaim to the whole parish and to the world that faithful discipleship costs, that sorting through to what God wants of us demands that we die to ourselves so we can rise together, transformed, into new life as a community of faith. Pastoral leadership gathered to discern the parish's vision, its direction for gospel ministry, allows the Spirit's life to penetrate deeply into each person and into the group, teaching them in the process the pattern of life Jesus has shown us.

EXTENDING HOSPITALITY

Hospitality is the pattern of life Jesus has shown us in his ministry among us, in his Eucharistic memorial, and in his revelation of our God as Trinity. It could very well be called by other names: the Divine Mercy, the expression of the Sacred Heart's abyss of love, solidarity, the tender care of *La Virgen morena*, living out the command to do justice, faithfulness to the great commandment to love God and neighbor, and so on. Yet the image of hospitality, so accurately expressive of Jesus' ministry of reconciling meals, brings home for us in the warmest way the essence of pastoral leadership's aim and the church's mission.

Hospitality affirms the equal dignity of persons even as it expresses in the accepting and being accepted, in the giving and receiving, the mutuality and interdependence we share as human beings. Hospitality celebrates unity in love even as it honors each person's distinct purpose in the exchange between host and guest. Hospitality enacts love, neighborly and self-emptying service; it enacts justice, in which we order our relationships rightly for the sake of building the common good; it enacts mercy, expressing divine forgiveness. Jesus extends hospitality throughout his ministry, and then across all space and time, because in hospitality we human beings are transformed in love, in justice, in mercy, as we meet one another and God face to face.

BUILDING TRUST

Pastoral planning, discernment decision making and hospitality in all things create the condition of possibility for Good News pastoral leadership. These three together build for us as a community of faith, over the long haul, trust in our leadership, trust in one another, and trust in God. In the end, around the third table of parish life where heaven and earth meet, it's all about trust.

— PROCESS QUESTIONS —

1. What do you think of the proposition that to-day's laity and more newly ordained clergy are on a collision course regarding the questions of authority and pastoral leadership in the parish?

2. What concerns do you have about your own parish community? What do you think is the top priority concern?

3. How would you approach these concerns as a council member? As a staff member? As pastor?

4. What are the first steps to building or enhancing trust in your own community?

CHAPTER 12

A Case Study: All Holy Angels Catholic Community

» Introduction

One way to reflect on how to bring hands together in pastoral leadership, and on what the proper approach might be for a pastoral council member, a pastoral associate, or a pastor, is to consider possibilities for transforming pastoral leadership through a modified case study method. All Holy Angels Catholic Community (AHACC), the parish cluster of St. Michael, St. Gabriel, St. Raphael, and Guardian Angels mentioned with its pastor Fr. Joe and secretary Dierdre in chapter 1 and chapter 9, offers a case through which we can explore how we might help bring about Good News pastoral leadership in a concrete parish situation.

What follows below lays out the history and current strains in the AHACC. Following that are a series of process questions to help you think through how a pastoral council member, a pastoral associate, or a pastor might approach bringing hands together for Good News pastoral leadership in the AHACC. The chapter ends with one person's perspective on how a pastoral council member, pastoral associate, or pastor might approach the same questions.

» All Holy Angels Catholic Community

HISTORY

The four parishes of the AHACC stretch across two counties of mountain and desert terrain in the southwest. The area, settled in the nineteenth century, is largely populated by Mormons, Evangelical Protestants, and people without religious affiliation. Catholics are a very small minority in a sparsely populated area of about 35,000 people across two counties.

The oldest of the parishes in Emperor County, St. Gabriel, was canonically erected in the little ranch town of Rivulet, near Big Butte National Park, in 1911. It has some seventy-four families today, many of whom are older and retired. In 1914, St. Gabriel at Rivulet took on St. Raphael's at Caterina, a little town in a small canyon twenty miles away, as a mission. Today with seventy-three households, St. Gabriel is the same size as St. Raphael's.

The largest of the parishes, Guardian Angels at Conquistador, was founded in 1943. Conquistador, Emperor's county seat, was founded in 1886 at the desert crossroads of mountain ranch territory, Big Butte National Park tourism, and the Totem Indian Reservation. St. Gabriel's at Rivulet, 20 miles east of Conquistador, took care of the Catholics there for many decades. Guardian Angels, which is also 10 miles southwest of St. Raphael's at Caterina, today is the largest of the four parishes with 377 registered households.

The smallest of the parishes, St. Michael's, is in Sunfield, a county away from the other three parishes and 33 miles away from the closest of them. The seat of Caterina County—the Caterina River winds through Emperor and Caterina counties—Sunfield is a small, dry-farming community on the high desert plains that grows sunflowers and pinto beans. St. Michael's Church was cut in two and moved to Sunfield in 1949 from the bottom of what is now the Caterina River Reservoir. A mission of Conquistador ever since and the only Catholic community in Caterina County, St. Michael's at Sunfield has thirty-five families.

The differences of geography, demography, and history among the towns and parishes make for considerable differences among the faith communities. These differences are accentuated by the strong pioneer independence that permeates the West, the self-reliance nurtured by ranch and desert territory, and the struggle for Catholic identity in an area where other religious traditions, or none at all, dominate. Added to the mix during the last fifteen years is the influx of California and Texas retirees. During the last five years, the area has also experienced an influx of Mexican migrant workers serving in local agriculture, restaurants, and hotels. The whole area is also weak economically; the few young people who finish college usually leave the area because they cannot make a living.

SINCE THE CLUSTERING

These four churches of 550 households became All Holy Angels Catholic Community in 1986. Since that time they have had five pastors and one interim administrator, with four part-time assistants tossed into the mix here and there. The pastors have been of varied ages, ideological stripes, and cultural backgrounds. One stayed seven years. One died after a few months.

The terms of the others fell in between. Two of the part-time assistants were retired and have died. Another part-timer was in the area on a family leave and one came fresh from Mexico. The AHACC is located at the very farthest end of the diocese, six hours away from the bishop.

The bishop asked Fr. Joe, a superior in his religious order, to take the parishes as a personal favor. Because Fr. Joe is fluent in Spanish and was willing to secure a Mexican priest from his order to help out, the bishop felt confident that the Spanish-speaking community would be cared for more adequately. Though the previous pastor had a bilingual Mass once a month, the bishop hoped for more. Fr. Joe committed himself to provide it.

THE MAJOR ISSUES
Money
Because of the local economy, money remains a central concern for the AHACC. Collections have been steadily modest, dipping during the 1997-2002 controversial pastorate of Fr. Ken. In nineteen years, none of the pastors has preached stewardship.

Every year, however, the parishes conduct a drive to meet their obligations to the diocese's Annual Catholic Appeal. This collection, taken up for the diocese to pay the parish's assessment (the diocesan tax levied to pay for the Chancery and other diocesan ministries), receives major attention each year because the diocese bills the parish monthly for the assessment, insisting on payment...or else! The press for contributions to the Annual Catholic Appeal, then, is effectively a stewardship appeal. The approach to the collection has very little grounding, however, in a theology of stewardship. The spirituality of stewardship has never been nurtured.

Lack of Staff

Because money is tight, the parishes have little staff. Only the parish secretary, Dierdre, works full-time. The parish business administrator and religious education coordinator are both part-time, each a mere five hours per week. Volunteers oversee worship in each parish, and a four-community liturgy committee discusses various liturgy planning concerns. The liturgy committee does a mite of spiritual formation. Pastoral care is done by the pastor and parochial vicar; it consists of requested pastoral visits, a Mass each week at the Rivulet and Conquistador nursing homes, and rounds in Conquistador's hospital. The Catholic Daughters in Conquistador, the Altar and Rosary in Rivulet, the Knights of Columbus in both, and small groups of parishioners in the others, provide stimulus for community building. As is usually the case, the women are far more effective in this ministry than the men, and have considerably more funds.

Unfocused Governance

The four-community council, which meets monthly on varying days depending on Fr. Joe's schedule, focuses on committee reports. Beyond reports, the councils tend to review physical facilities questions about the four plants. What repairs ought to be done and what money spent become major council discussions from time to time. The meetings are open, too, so sometimes parishioner agitation or complaint about this or that matter takes considerable council time.

The Spanish-Speaking Community: What is Unity Among Us?

The presence of the Spanish-speaking community, and the pastoral care they are receiving, vexes some members of the AHACC, particularly members of Guardian Angels at Conquistador. This vexation ostensibly has two levels: one relative to the Spanish-speaking community and one relative to the Mexican parochial vicar.

Fr. Joe has allowed the parochial vicar, Fr. Fernando, to exercise considerable authority in the Spanish-speaking community. Effectively, he is their pastor. While Fr. Joe maintains that the goal of the Spanish-speaking community ministry is to integrate them into parish life, Fr. Fernando holds a very tight rein. He steers them away from AHACC activities and toward establishing their own worship customs, catechetical programs, sacramental preparation requirements, and social events. He is not always successful in this endeavor, but that is nonetheless his orientation. The Spanish-speaking community—which the priests believe numbers two hundred people at full complement, but garners only sixty persons for Sunday Mass—even has its own Easter Triduum liturgies at Conquistador.

Coming from a village and Indian background, Fr. Fernando's behavior stirs some resentment among Mestizo and big-city Mexicans in the community. It also creates some inner conflict for people who are becoming increasingly acculturated as Americans and whose children know English well. At the same time, they find it hard to let go of their deep attachment to traditional Mexican veneration for Catholic clergy and respect for their every directive. Fr. Fernando's approach, therefore, grates against the sensibilities of some members of the Spanish-speaking community, annoys the land grant Spanish Catholics whose families have lived in the territory for hundreds of years and irritates those Anglos who hold "one community in Christ" as the ideal for their parish community.

Second, though Fr. Fernando is youthful, a humble man with a radiant smile and seemingly gentle disposition, he speaks very little English quite poorly and demonstrates no interest in improving his skills. Even his cell phone message is exclusively in Spanish. While Fr. Joe chooses to ignore this reality and himself speaks with Fr. Fernando in Spanish, Anglo parishioners across the parish, though they like Fr. Fernando personally, resent the incomprehensibility of his preaching and presiding. Parish youth in particular have withdrawn from Sunday Mass participation because of it, which alarms the older generations.

Indeed, What is Unity Among Us?

Because of the distance among the parishes, parishioners often struggle with these questions: Are we one community? Or are we one community with four sites? Or are we four communities? Or are we five communities? These questions are not being resolved.

In the time since the 1986 clustering, the first two pastors and the interim administrator addressed these questions very little. They treated the AHACC as four little parishes with one priest. The questions were surfaced strongly, however, during Fr. Ken's pastorate from 1997-2002. Though he was neither carefully articulate about it, nor politically astute, Fr. Ken took a particular stand on the AHACC: Guardian Angels at Conquistador ought to function something like a cathedral church for all four parishes. Major liturgical celebrations, catechetical sessions, and social events for the whole community were held at Guardian Angels. The Rivulet rectory was sold during his pastorate and the money was used to pay for a new rectory at Conquistador. The old rectory there was turned into a religious education space. Fr. Ken centralized much of the AHACC's ministry in Conquistador as well.

This stance won some hearts, particularly at Guardian Angels in Conquistador. It alienated others, particularly the people at St. Gabriel's in Rivulet, who are still angry their rectory got sold, and St. Raphael's in Caterina, who thought Fr. Ken self-absorbed and secular in his attitudes. St. Michael's at Sunfield, the smallest and farthest distant community up in Caterina County, ignored the fracas and continued to do as it wished. The pain of this experience—pushing one clear answer to a fundamental parish identity question, and doing it by fiat and without discussion—persists across the parishes, and that in spite of a relatively plodding and traditional three-year pastorate following Fr. Ken's and preceding Fr. Joe's.

Preserving the Pastor's Power

In this complex situation, Fr. Joe came to the AHACC in 2006 believing that it still needed healing from Fr. Ken's pastorate. He arrived on the scene concerned to "bring people back to church." To this end, he added one Mass to the weekend schedule and four to the daily Mass schedule. On Fridays, three Masses are celebrated, two at nursing homes and one at Conquistador. The added Sunday Mass he dedicated to the Spanish-speaking community.

A keen observer and highly intuitive about people, Fr. Joe immediately felt as if he just might have been assigned to pastor in a pool of sharks. His pressing question very quickly became: how does the pastor preserve his power in this situation? His answer was to withdraw his office from the parish center so he could preserve his power from being dominated by the ever-pressing Dierdre, and to restructure the pastoral council so he could get maximum information at the meetings (which had the added effect of paralyzing the council's power to act). Fr. Joe is secure as pastor of the AHACC and fully in control, indeed confidently so.

But now what?

— PROCESS QUESTIONS —

1. What would you diagnose to be the AHACC's foremost concern? Why?

2. How would you approach the AHACCs concerns as a member of the pastoral council? What actions are your best hope for success?

3. How would you approach these concerns as a pastoral associate? What actions are your best hope for success?

4. If you were appointed the AHACC pastor, what would you do about:

   The council's structure?
   How the council runs?
   Ministry to the Spanish-speaking community?
   The Mass schedule?
   Dierdre?
   Setting priorities among the gospel ministries?
   Getting the information and perspective you need in order to lead?

» One Perspective: Diagnosing the AHACC's Central Concern

Clarity of vision for the parishes, and effective power distribution among them, demands that pastoral leadership accurately diagnose the AHACC's first priority concern. What is it?

THE SECOND PRIORITY CONCERNS

Healing from Fr. Ken's pastoring style remains on the table in the AHACC. It may be there for some time to come. Still, it is a secondary concern in itself. His style, however challenging or abrasive it may have been, cannot account for the depth of feeling surrounding some parishioners' response to his pastorate. Getting people back to church cannot be the parish's first priority either. People left during Fr. Ken's pastorate because they had strong feelings about something. But what?

A convenient Mass schedule, even though it is unsustainable for the long run, helps people out at this time in the parish's life. As a pastoral tactic, however, it just might be a bandage on a broken leg. It does nothing for the break. Only setting the bone and giving it healing time will get the patient walking again.

Fr. Joe does need to preserve the pastor's power so the parishes can work together as a church under the pastor's leadership. His methods, however, create more problems than they solve. They leave the council structure cumbersome and paralyzed, while Dierdre remains unsupervised and flailing about. Forward movement for the AHACC is stopped, and ministry effectiveness is largely the accidental result of essentially directionless scattershot.

Integrating the Spanish-speaking community into the whole parish and American Catholic life is a high value. Fr. Fernando's methods, however, also create more problems than they solve, fracture the Spanish-speaking community itself, and distance it from the rest of the parish community. They pose some risk of fracturing Guardian Angels in time, if not the whole AHACC. His failure to learn English adequately pours salt on the wound for the 90 percent majority of parishioners who are Anglo.

Money usually takes care of itself if a parish is well led, parishioners trust pastoral leadership, and the pastor preaches the spirituality of stewardship.

So, what's the real, top priority concern for the AHACC?

THE TOP PRIORITY CONCERN

The first concern in this particular clustered parish situation is the ecclesiological matter of the parish's identity, its meaning as church. The core concerns the AHACC needs to face are the vexing questions surrounding the clustering itself: Who are we if we are connected with these other parishes? What does this connection mean? What is unity among us as a people of faith if we are scattered across two counties and worshipping at four sites?

Fr. Ken's pastorate uncovered the immense importance of these questions. They underlay the divergent convictions and strong feelings among parishioners that brought tumult to his pastorate. Fr. Fernando's pastoral methods, and lack of commitment to learning English adequately, chafe in the AHACC and threaten its unity because they highlight exactly the same questions.

Who are we as church? How do we do church together? These are the AHACC's central questions. The fundamental issue is identity. What that looks like, however, will most likely evolve and change across the years as demographics shift in Empire and Caterina counties, and in the parishes. Final answers to the AHACC's first questions, in other words, are probably beyond reach because any answers discerned will likely be temporary.

The process of reflecting on the questions and pondering their ramifications, however, matters vitally. Ongoing pastoral planning—engaging pastoral leaders and parishioners widely and continually in reflecting on the AHACC's identity, image, direction, and accomplishments—can be the ever-in-process resolution of the AHACC's first concern. Only the continual process of planning itself will help make room in the AHACC's life for the ever-changing answers to its identity.

With the top priority concern properly focused, pastoral leadership has grist for vision-establishing and vision-evolving pastoral planning as well as consensus-building direction and redirection. Pastoral leadership will also, within the process, be able to firm up the AHACC's commitment to the divine hospitality in all of parish life, and open the four faith communities and the AHACC as a whole to ever more trusting relationships with one another and with God. In simplest terms, the AHACC can be an especially pregnant sacrament of the Church universal in our age. Ongoing engagement with the questions, coupled with high quality gospel ministry day by day, is the AHACC's identity, and it needs to be helped to receive, accept, bless, and express that.

» Approaching the Top Priority Concern from Three Positions

A PASTORAL COUNCIL MEMBER'S APPROACH

The pastoral council structure Fr. Joe has set in place inhibits effective pastoral planning. Numbering in excess of fifteen people, comprising elected members as well as organization, club, and committee chairs, this council structure blunts the likelihood of efficient planning. The structure deserves careful reconsideration. At the same time, it might stay in place or go depending on the structure of the pastoral planning process.

If a pastoral council member were to urge planning and the council were to approve it, Fr. Joe would likely let it happen. Though he is reserved about distributing his power, he feels secure in it. He also prefers to keep peace. He may very well see the pastoral planning process as a constructive step in the parishes' life. While he would not lead it, and would probably hold himself somewhat aloof from it in meetings, he would likely support it.

If the whole council decided to be the planning group, assuming a doubling of their meetings, that would likely extend the planning process. In this situation, however, the larger group might help insure the possibility of building a broader consensus in the parishes.

If the council decided that a committee would plan, that also would extend the process because the council would tap into it only through reports and document approval discussions. Were this second option selected, the planning process would need to use focus group discussions at each of the parishes and across them, in an effort to build consensus among parishioners about the parishes' shared identity and vision in any given five-year period.

Either of these two planning options would probably preserve the current council structure. Proposing to change it might be worthwhile theoretically. Practically, however, Fr. Joe asked for this structure. Pursuing the question of change, on occasion at least, would test the waters, inviting the council and Fr. Joe to consider a more workable structure. Raising the issue would best be done in a very low-key fashion, however, since Fr. Joe might have some sensitivity around the question, especially now.

Fr. Joe would likely go along with discernment decision making if the council approved it as a method, especially if the council did so for itself and all other pastoral leadership groups. The trick would be getting Fr. Joe's participation in the discernment process. Moving forward with discernment decision making would require, at the very least, Fr. Joe's acquiescence to affirming the decisions such a process would produce. That may challenge him. Because of his security as pastor, though, he is likely to acquiesce.

Under the circumstances, these accomplishments would be enormously significant for a pastoral council member, and worth the risk of the attempt. These changes hold great hope of bringing the community together in purpose for the long run, even if they promise some tumult in the short run.

Pressing for these changes from outside the council, though the meetings are public, would have minimal effectiveness. That tactic just might inspire personal dismissal and quietly stubborn resistance from Fr. Joe, and hostility in some council members. Outside pressuring also risks council fracture.

A PASTORAL ASSOCIATE'S PASTORAL LEADERSHIP APPROACH

If competence, professionalism, transparent accountability, sound relationships, and the singular desire to do what God wants in ministry are all in place for a pastoral staff member, then Fr. Joe would probably be a supportive colleague. He would respond very well to being closely informed, having his confidence kept, and seeing ministry results. Building this relationship would be a pastoral associate's first priority.

Dierdre would be a major challenge as a colleague. Her method of operation as parish secretary, office manager, assistant to the pastor—however she may style herself on a given occasion—requires that a pastoral associate be in close and clear communication with Fr. Joe about Dierdre and the limits of her position. Clarity with Fr. Joe would allow the pastoral associate to ask from Dierdre what was needed from her, and to be specific with her about what is expected and what is not in relationship to the pastoral associate's ministry area. Dierdre's ostensibly fuzzy understanding of her own responsibilities allows her, in her mind, access to anything she chooses. A pastoral staff colleague would need to remain constantly vigilant about Dierdre's temptations to overstep her limits and to invite other staff members and parishioner volunteers to step over theirs. Clarity with Dierdre about her limits, even if in relationship with only one ministry area, would actually help her and the whole parish staff. Fr. Joe cannot be relied upon to face directly limiting and supervising Dierdre.

Taking advantage of the pastoral staff meeting could signifi-cantly help the entire staff, especially Fr. Joe, since the staff is so small. Raising the fundamental questions about the parishes' mission would help focus everyone, and lead eventually to their feeling more comfortable in the group. Staff meetings are infre-quent, however, because Dierdre likes them so much for her own purposes. Fr. Joe, therefore, steers clear. Most influence in staff, consequently, would need to be exerted in personal con-versations. That influence might be considerable.

A strong ministry commission example would likely have a major impact on the whole AHACC. The parishes are tightly knit and have sound across-parish communication structures. A Good News ministry commission, with members of each of the parishes on board, could bring about significant change in the long run.

THE PASTOR'S APPROACH
A pastor has great freedom to act. The pastor of the AHACC would need to act on several fronts simultaneously.

Changing the Council
The pastoral council needs to begin pastoral planning and im-plement discernment decision making, which would require doubling the number of meetings they have per year and clos-ing them to parishioner visitors. The pastor can easily request

this shift in council purpose and practice, and expect it to be implemented. The pastor also needs to invite the council to cut back membership to "elected" members only, not constituency representatives, so it will become a vision-building group and an effective forum for reflecting on the parishes' major questions about identity: Who are we if we are connected with these other parishes? What does this connection mean? What is unity among us as a people of faith? How do we choose to express our unity and our singularity? This change would gradually build trust for the whole parish community over time, as long as the pastor was actively engaged in it.

Reshaping Ministry for the Spanish-Speaking Community

The pastor would also need to reshape the Spanish-speaking community's relationship to the whole parish. Currently that community operates independently, and momentum in the direction of separation shows no sign of abating.

Fr. Fernando needs to be thanked heartily for his service and assigned to a different parish. His pastoral leadership posture in the Spanish-speaking community and the parishes at large precludes his remaining on staff.

Occasional Spanish-language Masses, consistently bilingual major event celebrations, the honoring and highlighting of Mexican customs for important feasts and family celebrations, attentive pastoral care for Spanish-speaking families, the erection of a statue of Our Lady of Guadalupe in the Conquistador church, and Mexican parishioners sitting around the table of all pastoral leadership groups—these actions should more than adequately minister to this community and integrate it into the AHACC. Accomplishing these goals means that the pastor needs passable Spanish skills himself, or a strong, loyal Spanish-speaking pastoral leader to assist.

A New Mass Schedule

Bidding farewell to Fr. Fernando would necessitate a new Mass schedule sustainable for one priest. This shift, though burdensome for the parishioners and certainly a cause for some short-run disturbance, would be a helpful and realistic development.

Setting Administrative Staff Limits

On staff, Dierdre requires a carefully reshaped ministry description that clearly delineates her responsibilities and duties. At this point, its emphasis would effectively be on limiting her. The pastor would need to hold her strictly accountable for fulfilling a revised ministry description, and proceed with progressive discipline if she fails. This way of supervising her would leave Dierdre the choice of whether or not she wishes to be employed by the AHACC.

The pastor moving his office into the parish center would greatly help staff supervision and markedly bolster the AHACC's sense that the pastor cares. So would his establishing his own telephone line and answering service.

Expanding Pastoral Staff

Beyond the ongoing pastoral planning process, high quality gospel ministry day-to-day needs to be the pastor's focus and commitment.

The AHACC desperately needs to ground its community experience in vibrant worship. To this end, the pastor needs to invite the councils to consider hiring a full-time pastoral staff member in liturgy and liturgical music, or perhaps halving such a full-time position with religious education. This position's role in AHACC liturgy would be to plan the weekly and seasonal liturgies, train all liturgical ministers and musicians, play at Eucharist, cantor, structure liturgical celebrations outside Mass, assist with sacramental preparation and the RCIA, and help with liturgical catechesis in religious formation programs. If the AHACC can come forward with Sunday stewardship enough to fund this position, rich and transcendent worship, coupled with strong preaching, would do most to open the parishes to the Holy Spirit's transforming power.

Religious and spiritual formation in the AHACC has been weak historically. The pastor needs to continue to encourage and support total community catechesis, a program already building in the AHACC, hinged on the *Generations of Faith* model. These gospel ministries demand the pastor's careful and focused attention so the religious and spiritual formation ministry can grow and flourish in a community hungry for them.

It would be wise for the pastor to establish a group of volunteer pastoral associates from among each community's natural leaders. Each community has one prominent member acknowledged as a leader. That person in each community—effectively a pastoral ministry coordinator in each parish—ought to be invited to be a pastoral associate within the whole. A member of the Spanish-speaking community might also be invited into the group as well, at least on an experimental basis.

Weekly informal conversations and formal semi-monthly meetings with this pastoral associate group would offer the pastor insight into each community and understanding about what's possible and what's not within and among the parishes. This group ministering prominently within the AHACC would go a long way toward building trust within and among the parishes, and would give the pastor eyes, ears, hands, and speech in parish leadership groups across the four parishes. This pastoral associate structure, coupled with council planning, would significantly shape the AHACC's future, whether that be as a single community or as several.

The Pastor's Presence

All of these actions on the pastor's part, coupled with his simple presence at almost every parish event and at every site, would preserve the pastor's power automatically and keep the AHACC financially stable. Financial stability would become increasingly secure with the pastor's preaching the theology and spirituality of stewardship.

» The AHACC's Future

Given the size of the territory—Rhode Island with a Catholic population of approximately 1,750—the likelihood of the four parishes becoming one is very small. The people from Sunfield regularly driving 33 miles from Caterina County to Conquistador, or 52 miles to Rivulet, would be far too demanding. The area's population is also growing, though at a snail's pace. The planning process needs to consider carefully the pace of that growth and what to do in the meantime.

In addition, the legal status of the four churches remains two parishes with two missions, and the parishioners at Conquistador and Rivulet especially are keenly aware of that point. So, the future of the AHACC is genuinely unclear; many possibilities could be on the table for planning.

Gathering concrete data about demographics, parish culture and parishioner hopes and desires, and processing these in an ongoing pastoral planning process, could enormously help the four parishes of the AHACC to address their most vexing questions, and shape their answers, even if these answers will continue to shift and change as the years progress.

» Our Hope

Bringing together the two hands of pastoral leadership—laity and ordained—is a challenge of vital importance for our future that must be met. Only by working together can we heal the cultural and personal rifts that keep us from exercising Good News pastoral leadership freely and joyfully.

Today, as ever, our sacred and venerable Catholic tradition offers us everything we need to soar with the Spirit. Ours is but to give ourselves over in collegial ministry to pastoral planning that reaches out in hope toward our future, to discernment decision making that remains ever alert to the Holy Spirit's wind and fire among us, and to a gracious hospitality that mirrors the pattern of life Jesus has shown us. If we do these things, then we will be distributing our pastoral leadership power well and rightly, thereby building trust and keeping that trust for the sake of our gospel mission to the world.

The Administrator and Trust

[People] should regard us as servants of Christ
and administrators of the mysteries of God.
The first requirement of an administrator is
that he prove trustworthy.

» I CORINTHIANS 4:1

Basic Parish Governance Policies

The following offers a sample of a parish's basic governance policies. These are from Our Lady of Peace Catholic Community in Minneapolis, Minnesota.

» Pastor

(Canon #519) The Pastor is the proper shepherd of the parish entrusted to him, exercising pastoral care in the community entrusted to him under the authority of the diocesan bishop in whose ministry of Christ he has been called to share; in accord with the norm of law he carries out for his community the duties of teaching, sanctifying and governing, with the cooperation of other presbyters and deacons and the assistance of lay members of the Christian faithful.

GENERAL NOTES

- The Pastor is accountable to the Archbishop as both Shepherd of the Local Church and Chair of the Corporate Board.

- The Pastor, who is corporate vice-president, is accountable to the Corporate Board.

- The Pastor is responsible for all matters of faith and morals, law, personnel, property, and finances in the parish community.

- The Pastor must act according to the norms of the Code of Canon Law, the Particular Law of the Archdiocese of St. Paul and Minneapolis, and Civil Law.

- The Pastor's authority is shared with parish leadership groups. The role of these leadership groups and their relationship to the Pastor is described below.

» The Corporate Board

Minnesota Statutes, Section 315.15, governs the formation of a parish corporation. The Archbishop associates himself with his Vicar General, the Pastor of the parish, and two lay members designated by the Archbishop, the Vicar General and the Pastor, or a majority of them, to form the corporation by signing and filing a Certificate of Incorporation (Articles of Incorporation) with the Secretary of State of the State of Minnesota, and recording a copy thereof with the County Recorder of the county of its location. These five persons constitute the corporation and, according to the Certificate of Incorporation, have power to transact all business of the corporation.

GENERAL NOTES

- The two lay members of the corporation serve for two-year terms and their successors are selected by the Archbishop, the Vicar General, and the Pastor, or by a majority of them.

- The Archbishop, by reason of his office, is President, and the Pastor of the parish, by reason of his office, is Vice-President and Chief Executive Officer of the corporation. The Secretary and Treasurer of the corporation are chosen from the members of the parish.

- The Certificate of Incorporation and the Bylaws adopted by the parish corporation provide for the five members of the corporation to constitute the board of directors.

SPECIFIC NOTES

- The Corporate Board must approve:
  Sale, purchase, mortgage, or gifts of real estate.
  Granting of easements.
  Lease or rental agreements.
  Stock transfers or sales.
  Major capital improvements or renovations.
  New construction.
  Major service contracts for more than $15,000.
  Borrowing of money.

» The Pastoral Council

(Canon #536)…a pastoral council is to be established in each parish; the pastor presides over it, and through it the Christian faithful along with those who share in the pastoral care of the parish in view of their office, give their help in fostering pastoral activity.

The pastoral council possesses a consultative vote only and is governed by the norms determined by the diocesan bishop.

GENERAL NOTES

- The Pastoral Council is a consultative body responsible

for advising the pastor regarding the focus, guidance, and monitoring of all parish ministries.

- The Pastoral Council is subject to the "Guidelines for Parish Pastoral Councils" of the Archdiocese of St. Paul and Minneapolis.

- The Pastoral Council

...participates in the responsibility for pastoral ministry and not just the administration of the parish. Its purpose and goals are extensive. It should research the needs, the ideas, the hopes, the life and activity of the people of God, so that the whole parish community can effectively carry out the mission of the parish and fully participate in the ongoing conversion that is central to its life. The Parish Pastoral Council should constantly evaluate the parish in its conformity to the gospel and those constitutive elements of the gospel which call for understanding the implications of justice. In this sense, the Parish Pastoral Council shares in the decision-making process which assists the pastor in carrying out the leadership role that is his within the parish.

("Guidelines for Parish Pastoral Councils")

SPECIFIC NOTES

- The Pastoral Council is the oversight body for all parish planning.

- The Council is responsible for advising the pastor on any matters which he brings before it, including matters regarding law, property, finances, and personnel.

- The Pastoral Council, and any individual within it, is free to raise issues and concerns to the pastor for his and/or the Council's review.

- Parishioners generally are free to raise issues and concerns to the Pastoral Council, by letter or personally, for the Council's review.

- The Pastoral Council must make a recommendation regarding:

    Sale, purchase, or mortgage or real estate; or acceptance of gifts of real estate.

    Granting of easements.

    The general terms of the lease or rental of property.

    Major capital improvements or renovations.

    New construction.

    Major service contracts for more than $15,000.

    Borrowing of money.

    The yearly budget.

    The major policies regarding the focus, guidance, and monitoring of each and all parish ministries.

    The long-range plan for the parish.

    The long-range plan of each ministry in the parish.

    The creation of a new ministry position.

    The Pastor's yearly goals and periodic ministry review.

» The Administrative Council

(Canon #537) Each parish is to have a finance council which is regulated by universal law as well as by norms issued by the diocesan bishop; in this council the Christian faithful, selected according to the same norms, aid the pastor in administration of parish goods…

GENERAL NOTES

- The Administrative Council is a consultative body responsible for advising the pastor regarding the focus, guidance, and monitoring of parish administrative ministries.

- The Administrative Council assumes extensive responsibilities in advising the pastor regarding the areas of personnel, property, and finances, including budget, endowment, stewardship, and other forms of giving.

SPECIFIC NOTES

- The Administrative Council is the focusing, guiding, and monitoring body for parish properties and monies.

- The Administrative Council makes recommendations to the pastor on any matters that he brings before it, including matters regarding law and personnel.

- The Administrative Council, and any individual within it, is free to raise issues and concerns to the pastor for his and/or the Council's review.

- Parishioners generally are free to raise issues and concerns to the Administrative Council, by letter or personally, for the Council's review.

- The Administrative Council must make a recommendation to the Pastoral Council regarding:

  Sale, purchase, or mortgage of real estate; or acceptance of gifts of real estate.

  Granting of easements.

  Lease or rental agreements.

  Major capital improvements or renovation.

  New construction.

Major service contracts for more than $15,000.

Borrowing of money.

The yearly budget.

The creation of a new ministry position.

The policies regarding the focus, guidance, and monitoring of the parish administration ministries.

» The Ministry Staff

The parish ministry staff comprises Pastoral Staff, Administrative Staff and Teaching Staff.

PASTORAL STAFF

General Notes

- The Pastoral Staff are those ministers who have oversight of a ministry in the parish, supervise other ministers, and set and monitor a budget area.

Specific Notes

- The Pastoral Staff works in a close collaborative relationship with the pastor and the rest of the Pastoral Staff. They share with the Pastor the pastoring ministry of the parish community.

- The Pastoral Staff must make a recommendation regarding:

    The major policies regarding the focus, guidance, and monitoring of the ministry for which he/she is responsible.

    The yearly budget in his/her own ministry area.

    The creation of a new ministry position for the parish.

ADMINISTRATIVE STAFF AND TEACHING STAFF

General Notes

- The Administrative Staff consists of the ministers collaborating together to support the major ministries of the parish: secretary, administrative assistant, maintenance supervisor and staff, Coordinators for Extended Day and Kitchen Service, etc. The Teaching Staff consists of those ministers employed to teach in the school ministry.

- The Administrative Staff and Teaching Staff consist of exempt and non-exempt staff.

Specific Notes

- The Administrative Staff and Teaching Staff members work in a close collaborative relationship with the Pastoral Staff member in the ministry areas of the parish each area.

- The Administrative Staff and Teaching Staff members are consulted in personnel and finance matters directly affecting their status or their ministry.

» Parish Leadership Groups

The leadership groups comprise all commissions advisory to a particular parish ministry and its staff, and their committees and subcommittees.

GENERAL NOTES

- The purpose of parish leadership groups is to focus, guide, and monitor a particular ministry area among the parish ministries.

- All parish leadership groups are, by their nature, advisory to the Pastor and a particular Pastoral Staff member in a given ministry area.

SPECIFIC NOTES

- All leadership groups need to be governed by a document descriptive of their purpose and parameters.

- All groups come to decision by consensus.

- All persons in all leadership groups must respect confidentiality with regard to matters of personnel, finances, property, and law.

- All monies which a parish leadership group oversees must be held in parish accounts with the pastor as signatory because all parish organizations and groups enjoy tax exempt status in light of their status as part of the Minnesota corporation "Church of Our Lady of Peace." Persons other than the pastor who hold on their own and are signatory on what ought to be parish accounts are tax liable for the funds in these accounts by the Internal Revenue Service.

APPENDIX 2

A Primer on Planning

» Introduction

What follows here is a "do-it-yourself" kit on planning based on a system developed by Dr. Robert G. Smith of Ohio State University. It is designed to help one person, or several people, plan anything they may want to plan. It is enormously helpful in a parish setting for doing whole parish or particular ministry area planning.

In planning we try to relate what we think we are doing with what we actually are doing so we can build on past and present trends to provide an intelligent framework for future development.

The following pages provide you with:

- An outline of the planning process
- An explanation of planning steps and terms.

Since the proof of the process outlined in these pages lies in the planning process itself, the best way to understand what follows and to test its worth is to take a single, simple area of present concern, work it through the planning process, and see what happens.

THE PLANNING PROCESS

The basic purpose of planning is to establish as high a correlation as possible between what we are thinking and what we are doing so that we may build on the recognition of past and present trends in our experience to provide an intelligent framework for future development.

BASIC STEPS   ## BASIC RESULTS

1. What do we think we are doing?   IDENTITY

DESCRIBE BASIC PURPOSE
 a. Describe basic beliefs
 b. Describe basic purpose (mission)
 c. Describe basic functions

2. What do we think conditions our doing it?   IMAGE

DESCRIBE RESOURCES AND CONSTRAINTS:
 a. Describe organizational structures
 b. Describe basic policies
 c. Describe basic characteristics
 d. Describe strengths
 e. Describe weaknesses
 f. Describe environmental factors
 g. Describe present assumptions

3. What do we intend to do?   DIRECTION

FORMULATE GOALS AND OBJECTIVES
 a. Establish general goals
 b. Establish specific objectives

4.How are we going to do it?   **ACCOMPLISHMENT**

PLANNING
   a. Collect necessary data
   b. Analyze trends and note
       planning gaps

PROGRAMMING
   a. Establish general strategies
   b. Design alternative programs
   c. Assign action responsibility

BUDGETING
Allocate resources

COORDINATING
   a. Coordinate activities
   b. Establish implementation schedule
   c. Initiate component planning

EVALUATING
Review, evaluate, and recycle the results

SUMMARY OF THE PLANNING PROCESS STEPS

Step 1: Describe Basic Reliefs, Purpose, and Function

A. BELIEFS

A listing of widely accepted convictions—not subject to further debate—that provide a foundation for planning. Beliefs frequently take the form of value statements.

B. BASIC PURPOSE (MISSION)

The broadest, most comprehensive statement possible describing continuing purpose.

C. BASIC FUNCTIONS

A listing of the separate, major, ongoing activities.

Step 2: Describe Resources and Constraints

A. ORGANIZATION

One or several charts describing the lines of authority, responsibility, accountability, and communication.

B. BASIC POLICIES

Listing of arbitrary but specific limits placed on the freedom of decision by those who make policy. Such policies cannot be changed or violated without changing the nature of the operation.

C. BASIC CHARACTERISTICS

Listing of the special identifying traits of the operation or group in question.

D. STRENGTHS

Positive evaluation of some of the above characteristics. Can be done by simply placing "+" before certain characteristics.

E. WEAKNESSES

Negative evaluation of some of the above characteristics. Can be done by simply placing "-" before certain characteristics, or a "+/-" of their evaluation is mixed or neutral.

F. ENVIRONMENTAL FACTORS

A description of the context within which the operation takes place, especially in terms of extrinsic factors which influence the operation and over which it has no control.

G. PRESENT ASSUMPTIONS

Problematical statements about the future that cannot be predicted by logical processes and are beyond the control of the operation, but which are taken for granted in planning.

Step 3: Formulate Goals and Objectives

A. GOALS

Quantitative or qualitative statements which express in broad terms what the operation intends to achieve. Since they are so broad as never to be fully realizable, goals express a continuing intention and, in this way, serve as a guide both in formulating specific objectives and in every subsequent step in planning. The formulation of goals marks a turning point in the planning process because it attempts to describe an operation in terms of what it ought to be.

B. OBJECTIVES

Specific ends towards which effort is directed and which represent a partial realization of a continuing goal. Objectives may be short-range, but they should be achievable within a certain time which is usually specified. Together with continuing goals, objectives inform all the subsequent steps of the planning process.

Step 4: Collect Data on Intended Objectives and Analyze Trends

A. DATA

The facts necessary to develop an information base for analysis of trends in areas specified by the goals and objectives.

B. TREND ANALYSIS

A study of the general lines of development over several years within areas specified by the goals and objectives. The projection of these trends into the future is based on the assumption that they will continue at the same rate unless modified by planning or by a change in environmental factors.

C. PLANNING GAPS

The planning gap refers to the difference between the development projected in terms of the trend analysis and that intended in terms of the goals and objectives.

Programs are subsequently devised to bridge the gap between the projected and the intended trends.

Step 5: Design Programs to Achieve Stated Objectives

A. STRATEGIES

Guidelines for employing resources to afford maximum support of goals and achievement of specific objectives.

B. PROGRAMS

An elaboration of strategies in terms of alternative possible approaches for achieving the stated objectives. It is important to explore and weigh all the options at this stage. Usually formulated as proposed projects.

C. ACTION ASSIGNMENTS

The responsibility for any action in planning and, more specifically, for the implementation of programs should be assigned to a specific person or group, along with a time for its accomplishment.

Step 6: Allocate Resources to Achieve Stated Objectives

A. ALLOCATE RESOURCES

Budgetary analysis and estimates of resources needed for new and improved programs.

Step 7: Coordinate and Schedule Activities to Achieve Stated Objectives

Step 8: Review and Evaluate Programs in Terms of Intended Objectives and Recycle the Results

APPENDIX 3

A Spirituality-Based Discernment Process

» Introduction

While the very nature of a parish leadership group's responsibilities demands openness to the Holy Spirit under the question "What is it that God wants of us?" there are times when a leadership group cannot come to immediate and clear consensus about an issue. In these moments, the nature of relationship in the Holy Spirit calls for entry into an ever deeper dialogue among the members of the group with the Scriptures, with our God who is a community in love and mission, with the tradition of the discipleship community, and with each other.

Each and every person is an equal partner in this dialogue. However, as the insights, attitudes, convictions, and values of the Word and the tradition meet with the insights, attitudes, interpersonal environment, and social environment of the divine and human experience within each individual, each has an absolutely unique gift to offer in decision making. Because of this reality, and because the decisions of the leadership group are intended to draw them more and more deeply into unity with God and the whole discipleship community, the leadership must always remember that it must be a people about the business of discerning the gifts and demands of our relationship with God.

Pastoral leadership groups, then, have no room for projections and power struggles, for nit-picking and silent deals, for huffiness or resignation to fate. Each member of the decision-making body is a disciple of the Lord. Each brings absolutely unique gifts to the group. Each is absolutely necessary to the discernment process of the group as a whole. It must be said at the same time that no individual is as smart as the discipleship community; the power of the Holy Spirit burns within and rushes over groups, revealing God's way in the assembled community. Consequently, unanimous consensus, discernment of spirits, is the way for the community of disciples to participate together in the mystery of God's ongoing revelation of himself to and within the community that is the Church. And while unanimity is an ideal that may not always be achieved, the discipleship community needs to make every effort to achieve it.

The particular discernment process outlined below is a way for a parish leadership group to be more certain of God's presence, to verify God's way, and to share fully, each disciple respecting every other's distinctiveness, all participating equally, in the business of discerning the gifts and demands of our relationship to God. This process finds its origins in the Jesuit community, and reflects the experience of St. Ignatius Loyola and his companions as they worked through the first questions about their community. It is substantially based on an article by Jesuit George Schemel and Sister Ruth Roemer ("Communal Discernment." *Review for Religious.* November-December 1981, pp. 825-36).

» The Discernment Process

THE ATTITUDES GROUNDING THE PROCESS

The discernment process must begin with three viable attitudes: faith, prayer, and freedom. The formal process itself, which builds on these attitudes, includes focusing the issue, separating the issues into cons and pros, then seeking areas of agreement and attempting consensus. Finally, the decision is monitored over weeks and months for both interior and exterior confirmation.

Faith

Faith rests in awareness. Faith includes awareness of God's acting in my individual life as well as awareness of how God works with me individually. God's work with each person has particular patterns, notes, and characteristics from which the person's holiness develops. Faith also includes awareness of how God works with the particular group in which the decision is being made. Each group has its own charism, its own common identity, which focuses its energy. At the time of discernment, this awareness should be heightened so that the decision is made explicitly in an atmosphere of faith. The question of all discernment is, at rock bottom: what does God want of us?

Prayer

Prayer demands an abiding sensitivity to those things which urge us close to God and nurture faith, hope, and love. It also demands an abiding sensitivity to those things which urge us away from God and nurture faithlessness, hopelessness, and indifference. Prayer demands as well a realization of both personal and corporate sinfulness, and a willingness to face our weakness honestly. Communion with God in prayer is the beginning, middle, and end of the discernment process. Dependence on and honesty before God are the attitudes that ground discernment.

Freedom

Freedom is the willingness to be responsive to whatever God may be asking. Freedom is detachment from the options placed before the group in the decision-making process. Freedom is an attitude of mind and heart that leads us to desire only pleasing God: wanting what God wants, receiving honor or scorn, riches or poverty, fame or being hidden, in whatever measure God wants it for us. The discernment process calls us to ask God for freedom from any hesitations or blocks in the decision-making process.

THE PROCESS ITSELF

With these three attitudes in place, the more formal aspects of the communal discernment process begin.

Focusing the Issue

Formulate the question to be considered in a simple manner. This step of the process demands study, research, evaluation, and working to get to the facts. It also demands reviewing the feelings and values of the group toward the issue at hand. In this step the group strives to move toward the clarities of the moment while sorting through the struggles within the group. This step is the beginning of learning to live with the discernment process as a whole as well as learning to live with its outcome. The results of this step should be a simple, declarative statement.

Separating the Issues into Cons, then Pros

Separating the issues into cons first, and then pros, is the next step of the process. Within this step, the members of the group need to work at being willing to look at both sides of the issue.

Cons are done first because they tend to disappear when they are done second. The process of separating the issues requires that, going around again and again in a circle, each member of the group offers a con. This continues until all, in their turn, have spoken all of the cons they think relevant. The same is then done for the pros. Equal time is given to both cons and pros. The purpose of this step is to uncover all of the reasons, and the real reasons, for the decision that needs to be made.

Seeking Areas of Common Agreement

The next step of the process is seeking areas of agreement. Sometimes the group may not agree on the whole of a particular course of action, but the articulation of their agreement on certain elements of the issue may help them to see more clearly the direction their consensus might take.

Reflection and Prayer

The process might also include setting time aside for quiet reflection and prayer if consensus is not readily achievable or if a stalemate seems to develop. If consensus is not achieved, the process may need to start again from the beginning. Perhaps the consensus might be that consensus is not possible surrounding this issue. In such a case, the group might focus on their agreement and reach consensus about how to handle the issue for further consideration. The group might also decide to drop the issue altogether. In any case, the purpose of this step is to achieve consensus.

Exterior and Interior Confirmation of the Decision

Finally, after a decision is reached it needs to be monitored over the next days, weeks, and perhaps months for the sake of its confirmation. If the decision is what God wants, then the group should experience harmony in the results of the decision both interiorly and exteriorly. Interior confirmation is the experience of peace and joy in the Holy Spirit after the decision is made. The decision is experienced as congruent, and those who decided are able to remain appropriately detached from the decision. Exterior confirmation is simply the reality check of the decision's working over time. This reality check includes the acceptance of the decision by the community and by the legitimate authority.

» When to Use the Process

Typically, consensus is readily achievable without the use of this process. Most of the issues considered by most groups do not have the moment, or sufficient controversy, to warrant so structured a process.

Over the years, however, I have known two exceptions. Both were campus ministry volunteer programs issues. One, at the College of St. Thomas, St. Paul, in 1978, had to do with the question: should volunteers receive academic credit for their volunteer work? The other, at St. John's University, Collegeville, in 1980, had to do with whether volunteers should receive any form of compensation, even token compensation, for their volunteer work. In both cases, the questions were perceived as central to the identity of the program. Both issues were debated hotly and with tears. The process worked. In the first instance, in fact, the adamant conviction and persuasive power of one person won over the whole of the group, who originally disagreed with her. In both instances, all were happy with the consensus decision!

As a rule of thumb, then, the full process needs to be used only with those issues that concern the very identity of the community or a particular ministry within it, or those issues in the community or a particular ministry that might be volatile. Ordinarily, it would be unnecessary to use the process in full. The elements of the process that need to be kept in mind in discernment are the attitudes of faith, prayer, and freedom that always need to ground consensus decision making. A most useful element of the process is the separating of the issue into cons first, then pros.

Only if all else breaks down, and unanimous consensus is seemingly impossible to achieve, would it make sense to take a vote. I have never had to face this circumstance. Others, however, have experienced such circumstances and found that the shift to voting, while terribly painful, has ultimately worked out. It worked out because of the monitoring step, which requires the decision-making body to return again to the basic decision. Typically, if a decision is right for a community, even those who have held back from agreeing with the original decision will likely come to eventual agreement.

» Conclusion

This discernment process is one of faith, prayer, freedom, and the plain hard work of placing the pastoral leadership group in God's hands for the decision-making process. Moreover, of all the elements of the process to remember, none is more critical than the ultimate question underneath any consensus decision: what does God want of us?

Sample Ministry Descriptions

Two sample ministry descriptions follow. While no ministry description is ever absolutely complete, these samples represent an effort to provide new and current staff as complete a picture as possible of what the ministry position demands. The first is a pastoral associate ministry description. The second is an administrative staff ministry description.

Position Title:
Pastoral Associate for Education/Principal

DATE: Summer

REPORTS TO: Pastor

FLSA STATUS: Exempt

SCHEDULE: 12 months, 40 hours per week

DIRECT REPORTS: School Faculty, Administrative Assistant, Maintenance Supervisor, Extended Day Coordinator, Athletic Director

PROVIDES WORK DIRECTION TO: Faculty, Administrative Assistant, Maintenance Supervisor, Extended Day, Athletics, School Ministry Commission

RECEIVES WORK DIRECTION FROM: Pastor

RESOURCE PERSON TO: Pastoral Staff

JOB PURPOSE: To lead the parish's school ministry in accordance with its mission statement.

GENERAL RESPONSIBILITIES: Employment in and by the Church is substantially different from secular employment. Church employees must conduct themselves in a manner consistent with and supportive of the mission of the Church. Their public behavior must not violate the faith, morals, or laws of the Church or the diocese such that it could embarrass the Church or give rise to scandal. It is expected that all employees respect Roman Catholic doctrine and religious practices. Reasonable accommodations for the religious practices of employees who are not Roman Catholic will be provided.

The position does not require that the employee be an active, participating Roman Catholic, though that is strongly preferred.

REPRESENTATIVE RESPONSIBILITIES:

Maintain student academic, technological, personal and spiritual growth towards excellence by: Reviewing the curriculum and working with the staff to develop it; keeping abreast of local and national resources, trends, and developments in education; overseeing standardized testing and the teacher curriculum committees; keeping abreast of student needs; developing and enforcing academic and spiritual standards of excellence; nurturing faith development of staff and students in collaboration with the parish's pastoral staff and diocesan education office resources; coordinating counseling services with the public schools and other agencies; evaluating the Extended Day Program for safety and compliance with state standards; reviewing the athletic program, policies, and the enforcement of such with the Athletic Director.

Manage and develop the school ministry's staff to reach professional excellence by: Developing and maintaining accurate, accountable ministry descriptions, including measurement standards and goals for professional growth/development; coaching and mentoring staff toward achieving goals; conducting and documenting annual reviews with each school staff member, including classroom observation of teachers; maintaining, updating and enforcing personnel policies in collaboration with the Pastor; conducting weekly staff meetings.

Promote and nurture the parish's identity by: Applying a Catholic educational vision to the daily operation of the school; providing weekly communications to students, faculty, parents, and the parish of school events and news; overseeing the flow and

distribution of all agendas and information for school meetings; working with the Development Committee in shaping
communications about the parish's school ministry for recruitment and general marketing purposes; communicating with
the diocese, the principals of the deanery, and local Catholic
high schools as well as elementary schools; recruiting and re-
taining a strong student population as well as teaching staff.

Build a strong team within the school by: Promoting and fostering
active participation and leadership among faculty, parents, advisory groups, etc.; overseeing and coordinating student activities
(Patrols, Student Council, recognition programs, graduation,
Catholic Schools Week, etc.); working with staff to recruit, train,
and help manage parent and parishioner volunteer ministries;
interacting daily with students in informal as well as formal settings; collaborating with the school ministry commission and
parents' association by attending meetings, setting agendas, etc.

*Build and nurture a collaborative relationship between the school
ministry and all of the parish's ministries by:* Consulting with
the Pastor in matters related to morals, faith (worship, religion
curriculum, sacrament preparation, and ethics), law, finances,
and personnel; building working relations among parish
committees (i.e. school ministry commission and parents'
association, etc.); collaborating with the Pastor and Pastoral
Staff in providing regular liturgical celebrations; reviewing and
developing the religion curriculum with the Pastor, Pastoral
Associate for Religious Formation, and the teachers; working
with the Director for Finances (in consultation with the
Pastor and School Ministry Commission) to develop a budget
and monitor expenses and income as related to the school
ministry; coordinating with the school ministry commission in
developing policies, long range plans, and enforcing/monitoring

the policies and plans; working with the commission to seek and develop resources for the school ministry (i.e. grants); participating in semi-monthly pastoral staff meetings and the annual calendar and planning sessions.

Maintain Administrative and Operational efficiencies by: Maintaining personnel files in collaboration with the Director for Finances and Pastor; providing substitute teachers as needed; developing the yearly calendar; ensuring compliance with OSHA standards; ensuring a clean, orderly, safe and secure facility; planning, overseeing, and monitoring the purchase of books and materials under state and federal programs.

Continue professional development by: Attending professional workshops, seminars, courses as mutually agreed upon with the Pastor; working with the Pastor to set performance goals; actively participating in own job review each Spring or as needed in accord with diocesan policies.

To be present where needed, ready to work, and on time for all scheduled hours by: Recognizing when situations require more effort, seeking approval to put in more time if needed, satisfying responsibilities in a timely manner, providing an example of punctuality and attendance, and generally assuring that all is ready and taken care of.

OTHER RESPONSIBILITIES: The responsibilities listed above are representative responsibilities intended to describe the general nature and level of work performed by staff members assigned to this position. It is not intended to be an exhaustive list of responsibilities and qualifications required of the position. More detailed listings of duties and tasks may be outlined in supplemental documents. Those preceded by an asterisk are essential functions of the job.

EMPLOYEE: *I have reviewed this ministry description and agree it is an accurate representation of the responsibilities of my job. I understand that as an organization's needs change my job will change.*

_____   _____

Employee signature   Date

SUPERVISOR: *I have reviewed the ministry description and agree that it is an accurate representation of the responsibilities performed in this position.*

_____   _____

Supervisor signature   Date

Job Title:
Pastoral Associate for Education/Principal

DATE: Summer

JOB QUALIFICATIONS:
Masters level education
Licensure as an administrator
Practicing Roman Catholic strongly preferred
5 years experience as an administrator

MENTAL DEMANDS:
Clear sense of what constitutes the Catholic identity of a school ministry
Strong interpersonal relationship skills with teachers, parents, and children
Strong administrative and organizational skills
Expertise at work with curriculum
Know Civil and Canon Law as it applies to Catholic schools
Excellent listening and communication skills
Able to work independently on routine matters, offer new ideas without fear and with flexibility
Ability to maintain confidentiality
Work well with others, demonstrating a positive and helpful attitude at all times

PHYSICAL DEMANDS:
Work 40 or more hours per week
Able to sit for long periods of time
Able to operate office equipment
Able to walk comfortably throughout the plant daily
Able to do some evening work for the sake of meetings

Position Title:
Maintenance Supervisor

DATE: Spring

REPORTS TO: Pastor

FLSA STATUS: exempt

SCHEDULE: 12 months, 40 hours per week

DIRECT REPORTS: Custodians

PROVIDES WORK DIRECTION TO: Custodians

RECEIVES WORK DIRECTION FROM: Pastor, Pastoral Associate for Education/Principal

JOB PURPOSE: To provide a well-running plant, a well-supervised custodial staff, and a clean, sanitary, safe, and aesthetically pleasing environment at the parish.

GENERAL RESPONSIBILITIES: Employment in and by the Church is substantially different from secular employment. Church employees must conduct themselves in a manner which is consistent with and supportive of the mission and purpose of the Church. Their behavior must not violate the faith, morals, or laws of the Church or the diocese, such that it can embarrass the Church or give rise to scandal. This position does not require that the employee be a Catholic. It is expected, however, that non-Catholic employees will respect Catholic doctrine and religious practices. Reasonable accommodations for the religious practice of non-Catholics will similarly be provided.

REPRESENTATIVE RESPONSIBILITIES:

Run the plant: Includes assessing all of the mechanical systems, keeping all mechanical systems in good running shape, structuring the necessary consultations when operations fail, taking bids for repairs or purchases, being available for all forms of repair, fix-up, and refurbishing as the need arises.

Supervise the custodial staff: To review and structure their yearly, monthly, weekly and daily schedules; to touch base with each twice daily during their shift, and as necessary otherwise, so as to maintain accountability and quality standards; to instruct them when their work is deficient; to offer regular review of their work; to be responsible, in consultation with the Pastor and Principal, for progressive discipline.

Be present where needed, ready to work as needed to meet responsibilities: Includes recognizing when situations require more effort, seeking approval to put in more time if needed, satisfying responsibilities in a timely manner, providing an example of punctuality and attendance, and generally ensuring all is ready and taken care of.

Oversee the completion of daily cleaning services on a scheduled basis: This includes vacuuming, sweeping, mopping, dusting, cleaning bathrooms, and cleaning kitchen areas. Participate in the work when necessary.

Oversee the disposition of trash and recycling: Make sure the custodial staff maintains the weekly trash and recycling removal schedule for all areas of the facility, and pick up debris around buildings and pick up trash or recycling as required.

Use all equipment in a safe manner: Maintain equipment in a fully operational manner.

Supervise keeping bathrooms clean and fully stocked: Keep an adequate stock of cleaning supplies in all areas to meet cleaning requirements.

Oversee grounds maintenance: Engage a service to perform lawn and grounds maintenance and supervise snow removal, salt and sanding in season. Participate in snow removal when necessary.

Oversee summer and off-time maintenance: These times will include washing windows, stripping and waxing floors, shampooing carpets, and polishing furniture.

Oversee room setups: When a room is reserved, supervise the set up of rooms prior to scheduled meetings; including setup of tables, chairs, and required equipment. Respond to additional meeting setup requirements requested by meeting participants. Participate in the work when necessary.

Oversee security: While buildings are being cleaned, be aware of the presence of other people and make sure they are in the building for a valid reason. Assure that buildings are locked and secured at the end of the day. Take security actions required to maintain safety and order.

OTHER RESPONSIBILITIES: The responsibilities listed above are representative of the job and are not inclusive. Those proceeded by "*" are essential functions of the job.

EMPLOYEE: *I have reviewed this job description and agree it is an accurate representation of the responsibilities of my job. I understand that as an organization's needs change, my job description will change.*

_____   _____
Employee signature   Date

SUPERVISOR: *I have reviewed this job description and agree it is an accurate representation of the responsibilities performed in this job.*

_____   _____
Supervisor signature   Date

Position Title:
Maintenance Supervisor

DATE: 12/2/2005

JOB QUALIFICATIONS:

Second Class Boilers license

Experience working as a custodian

Skills and interests in fixing mechanical systems

Able to accomplish tasks within allotted time

Must be responsible in carrying out high quality work

MENTAL DEMANDS:

Knowledge of mechanical systems

Knowledge of how to work well with subordinates and supervise them

Knowledge of how to work with company representatives making bids

Knowledge of how to work with contract workers

Knowledge of cleaning materials and chemicals, safe use of all materials

Knowledge of safe operating and maintenance of cleaning machines, such as vacuums and floor scrubbers

Ability to follow supervisor's instructions and to work independently on routine and regular assignments

Maintaining a positive and helpful attitude at all times, even during difficult times

PHYSICAL DEMANDS:

Work 40 hours per week

Good working techniques in lifting, pushing, pulling, and other motions are required—comfortable and able, at a minimum, of 75 pounds of lifting

Bibliography

Aquinas, St. Thomas. *Summa Theologica*. In "Great Books of the Western World." Volume II. New York: Encyclopaedia Britannica, 1993.

Cassian, John. *Conferences*. In "The Classics of Western Spirituality." Translated by Colm Luibheid. New York: Paulist Press, 1985.

Code of Canon Law: Latin-English Edition. Washington, D.C.: Canon Law Society of America, 1983.

Co-Workers in the Vineyard of the Lord: A Resource for Guiding the Development of Lay Ecclesial Ministry (Washington, D.C.: U.S.C.C.B., 2005). Internet version.

D'Antonio, William V., James D. Davidson, Dean R. Hoge and Mary L. Gautier. *American Catholics Today: New Realities of Their Faith and Their Church*. New York: Rowman and Littlefield, 2007.

Davidson, James D. and Dean R. Hoge. "Mind the Gap: The Return of the Lay-Clerical Divide." In *Commonweal*. Vol. CXXXIV, No. 20, November 23, 2007, pp. 18-19.

Dulles, S.J., Avery. *Models of the Church*: Expanded Edition. Garden City, NY: Image Books, 1982.

Flannery, O.P., Austin, Ed. *Vatican Council II: the Conciliar and Post Conciliar Documents*. Northport, New York: Costello Publishing Company, 1992.

Glynn, Dr. Lori. *Six Indicators of Effective Catholic Governance Structures.* Unpublished presentation. Availabe through Catholic Education and Formation Ministries Office, Archdiocese of St. Paul and Minneapolis.

Greenleaf, Robert K. *Servant Leadership: A Journey into the Nature of Legitimate Power and Greatness.* New York: Paulist Press, 1977.

"Guidelines for Parish Pastoral Councils." Clergy Bulletins. A publication to the pastors available through the Office of the Chancellor of the Archdiocese of St. Paul and Minneapolis.

Hoge, Dean R and Jacqueline Wenger. *Evolving Visions of the Priesthood.* Collegeville: Liturgical Press, 2003.

O'Meara, O.P., Thomas F. *Theology of Ministry.* New York/Mahwah, NJ: Paulist Press, 1999.

Papesh, Michael. *Clerical Culture: Contradiction and Transformation.* Collegeville: The Liturgical Press, 2004.

———. "Farewell to the Club." *America.* Vol. 186, No. 16, May 16, 2002, pp. 7-12.

Puhl, S.J., Louis J. *The Spiritual Exercises of St. Ignatius.* Chicago: Loyola University Press, 1951.

Rolheiser, OMI, Ronald. *The Holy Longing: The Search for a Christian Spirituality.* New York: Doubleday, 1999.

———. *The Restless Heart.* New York: Doubleday, 2004.

Schaef, Anne Wilson and Diane Fassel. *The Addictive Organization.* New York: Harper and Row, 1990.

Schemel, George, S.J., and Sister Ruth Roemer. "Communal Discernment." *Review for Religious.* November-December 1981, pp. 825-836.

Schulte, Raymond. "Performance Evaluation: An Experience of Hell or a Taste of the Kingdom." *MP&R: The Ministry Planning & Review System for Head of Staff and Members of Staff.* Chicago: The Center for Parish Development, 1998.

Special Report: National Parish Inventory. Center for Applied Research in the Apostolate. Washington, D.C.: Georgetown University, 2000.